Faith Beyond Despair

Elias Chacour became Archbishop of Galilee in 2005. The Mar
Elias Educational Institutions, of which he is President, have
been promised accreditation for the University and subsidies
for the schools. But none of these promises has yet been honoured by the Israeli government, and the institutions rely on
voluntary donations in order to survive. Donations in the UK
are forwarded by the Elijah Trust, Registered Charity No.
1063263, to which all fees and royalties arising from this publication have been assigned.

More information may be obtained from The Elijah Trust, 45
Howbury Street, Bedford, MK40 3QU, UK
www. elijahtrust.org.

Faith Beyond Despair

Building Hope in the Holy Land

Elias Chacour
Arab-Israeli Priest
Archbishop of Galilee

with Alain Michel
translated and edited by Anthony Harvey

CANTERBURY
PRESS
Norwich

© Elias Chacour 2008

Originally published in French in 2002 under the title
J'ai foi en nous by Editions des Presses de la Renaissance,
12 Avenue d'Italie, Paris

First published in 2008 by the Canterbury Press Norwich
(a publishing imprint of Hymns Ancient & Modern Limited,
a registered charity)
13–17 Long Lane, London EC1A 9PN

www.scm-canterburypress.co.uk

British Library Cataloguing in Publication data

A catalogue record for this book is available
from the British Library

ISBN 978-1-85311-906-4

Typeset by Regent Typesetting, London
Printed and bound by
CPI Bookmarque, Croydon, Surrey

Contents

I dedicate this work to all my Jewish and Palestinian brothers and sisters who have been martyred, and to their families who lament their loss. They all cry out with one voice: Enough of hatred and violence! The time has come to unite.

Preface

Alain Michel

Amid the fear and anguish that daily confront the men and women of Israel and Palestine, I asked myself: Was there any voice being raised that, like a light in the darkness, would speak of hope? It would have to be a credible voice, one that recognized the true value of both friend and enemy, the voice of one who had devoted his life to the struggle to make people recognize one another as human beings. This land is a garden of tears; yet there exist seeds of peace. There exist builders, people who will not let us despair, however desperate the situation; there exist peacemakers. A book series published by Presses de la Renaissance in France called 'Men of their Word' (*Hommes de Parole*) has found such peacemakers, and has committed itself to pass on to others its resolute option for peace amid the tumult of bad news and hopelessness. Peace is difficult, but it is not impossible. To believe in it is already to give it a chance.

Elias Chacour is one such man, a man both of riches and of poverty, but also a man with an obstinate and unquestionable will to fight for peace – real peace, the peace of the heart.

In Ibillin, in the college that he founded, or in his home, we have talked together for many hours, for long days and long evenings. He has told me of his life, his sufferings, his moments of despair and of loneliness, but also of his joys and especially of his hopes. This book is the result. Today I know with certainty that his struggle is truly a struggle for peace. It is a struggle that many may find hard to accept. Elias Chacour is a citizen of Israel; but since he is also and above all 'a man born as a baby in the image of God' (as he likes to say), he is equally a Palestinian Arab who speaks in the name of his people and shares their concerns.

Behind the acerbity and occasional extreme directness that he sometimes shows towards certain Israeli Jews, one can feel that his passion is to establish peace on the foundations of justice and integrity, spiritual courage and human transparency, and to continue working towards it in order never to give in to those who try to destroy it.

In the course of these last years I have tried to understand the suffering of both Palestinians and Israelis, and I can confirm that, contrary to what is said by those who are determined to encourage hatred and violence, the one desire of the majority of both populations is to achieve a truly just and fraternal peace. Their destiny is to reach agreement 'despite everything'.

Elias Chacour represents a living witness to this supposedly impossible co-existence in the Middle East, for he works along-side everyone and is accepted as much by the Israelis as by the Palestinians. He is a man who, despite the bitterness that his people's history might inspire in him, has constantly left such feelings behind him and worked for the reconciliation of the two 'blood brothers', as he calls them, the Israelis and the Palestinians.

This reconciliation begins in the school that he has founded at Ibillin, where Palestinian Christian and Muslim children, along with Israeli Jewish children, learn side by side under teachers who are equally mixed in race themselves. It is on these school benches that peace is being built, it is here that the Israel of Elias Chacour is taking shape, a land of peace where the children of God who still do not know each other may live together reconciled. For they all believe in the one God of the Bible, who was revealed to Abraham.

Elias Chacour is 'a man of peace in a country at war'. He is a man who seeks to live in peace and in the search for justice. He is a man obsessed by love for his country and for his people. The one thing which he tries to say is something inspired by the message of the one who has guided him throughout his childhood and throughout his life, Jesus Christ. To present him as 'another man from Galilee' is not to compare him with Christ, but to acknowledge his determination to follow Christ. Elias Chacour would wish that these new men of Galilee, the Galileans of the present and of the future, whether Palestinian, Muslim, Jew or Christian, should speak the language of God – the language, not of war, of fear, or of revenge, but of humanity. His desire is for everyone to become a new human being. This is the message of love he would wish to see spreading throughout the world.

Alain Michel

Introduction

Elias Chacour
Another Man from Galilee

Alain Michel

Elias Chacour was born in Bar-am, a very poor village in Galilee. He was the youngest of a Christian family of Palestinian Arabs, with four brothers and a sister. The inhabitants of Bar-am lived in great poverty, but they were happy and united. Elias Chacour grew up at the heart of a community that lived around the church and under the influence of the parish priest. Far from asphalt roads and electric light, his life was certainly simple, but it was a simplicity drenched in a great deal of happiness. Later, when he reached adulthood, he used to say that he lived in the company of his 'compatriot' – meaning Jesus Christ. In his childhood he was known for his games, and known also for the way he had appropriated certain trees surrounding his family house. He had made his own the largest fig tree, where he loved to hide and stay for long hours quite quietly, seated in the shade of the branches. It was his favourite tree because of the variety of figs it produced. Then there was a vine, which climbed up the olive tree, and this provided food and drink. That was all he needed to feel happy. Unfortunately, his happiness did not last. When he was eight years old he had to leave his village and follow his people into the exile that the war imposed on them. For several months he and his family slept under trees or in caves, their only possession a blanket to protect them from the cold. They took refuge in a village close to their own. All seven of them lived in a single small room that had belonged to a Lebanese family, which itself had been forced to leave Palestine to go and live in Lebanon. Despite all this, they counted themselves lucky, for the roof of their house was of concrete, unlike the others which were less robust, being of baked mud. His parents remained in the village of Jish until 1987.

Elias Chacour's father had always wanted one of his children to become a priest. For him it was as if he was offering one of his children to God. None of his brothers had been willing, so there was only Elias. Soon after having been expelled from his village, his father met the bishop. Instead of asking him to understand their sufferings, to help him to claim his rights and to return to his village, his father, in Elias's presence, said to the bishop in front of everyone, 'My Lord, I have a son, I would like him to become a priest.' The bishop replied, 'Send him to me.' Which is how Elias Chacour found himself in the orphanage in Haifa. There he began to eat the bread of the poor, the bread of orphans. He was taught at school by the Christian brothers. It was like a family.

In 1956 his bishop, Patriarch Maximos V, began to build a small seminary in Nazareth, and transferred the brothers to it. At that time the seminary was quite primitive: there were neither doors nor windows, for there was not enough money to complete the building. Elias Chacour remembers very well that first year, when a wave of cold weather descended on Nazareth and they had to close up the openings with blocks of stone and cardboard.

He finished at the secondary school in 1958, and the bishop

sent him with his friend Faraj Nakléh to continue their studies abroad. The bishop had the choice of sending them to Rome or to Paris. From a middle-eastern perspective, Rome seemed like a city much too closed in on itself, too traditionalist. Paris attracted them more, and fortunately the bishop chose to send them there. When they arrived in Paris they studied at Saint Sulpice and heard lectures from Cardinal Daniélou at the Institut Catholique. Elias completed his studies in 1965 and was ordained deacon in Saint Julien le Pauvre, the small Greek-Catholic church in Paris. He and his friend Faraj then returned to Nazareth on 24 July 1965. It was a cause of celebration for the whole diocese, since they were the first priests to be ordained for 24 years. Their dearest wish was to remain poor, and God seemed to have heard them, for he had stripped the church of everything.

A few months after their ordination, a retreat was organized for priests. The bishop, who was very proud of his new recruits, made them sit next to him. When the older ones had finished lauding him and praising him to the skies, representing him as a first-class politician and leader, he wanted to hear a word from his young priests. It was for Faraj to make a speech, but nothing would make him do so. He refused. So Elias had to speak on his own, and he said to the bishop, 'You are a political prince-bishop, and in you Israel has a man of unequalled talent; but none of that impresses me. What would impress me would be to see this same man follow the example of his master, to see him wash the feet of his priests and his parishioners and kiss them. If you do that, then I will think of you as a man of God. But as long as you do not do it, nothing that you do will have any value in my eyes.' It seems likely that these words made a considerable impression on the bishop.

Later on, this same prelate sent Elias to study at the Hebrew University in Jerusalem. He said he was ashamed of his own ignorance, which prevented him from conversing with his Israeli guests when they talked to him about St Thomas or Gregory of Nazianzus. He wanted Elias to study so that he could meet them on their own ground. Elias Chacour decided to specialize in the Talmud and the Old Testament. At the university he learnt Aramaic, Syriac and Ugaritic, which were necessary to qualify for his master's degree. The two years he spent in that university were the most important of his life, more enriching even than his six years in Paris. He learnt what it meant to be 'an Arab' and 'a Palestinian' in a hostile environment. He learnt also the importance of dignity. It was there that he became aware that despite the situation of his own country he could make real friendships with Jews and that they could appreciate each other and even love each other. This was particularly the case with professors Verblovski, Talmon and Flusser. It was there that he learnt to know the Jewish world, Jewish theology, the Jewish Bible and the way in which his Jewish brothers understand and interpret it.

In 1970, overcome by despair at the Palestine–Israel, Jewish–Palestinian problem, he took a plane and sought refuge in Geneva, where he took the job of assistant to a university professor and lectured on ecumenism, pluralism and dialogue. He had fled to Geneva thinking that in this way he could get away from the problem; but he was deluding himself. He imagined the problem to be outside himself, but in reality it was an integral part of himself. He soon came back to Israel, and devoted himself to the social and economic development of Arab villages. His first project was the building of municipal libraries. Today there are eight of them, holding 150,000 books. The second of his projects was organizing holiday camps for the children of these villages. The first camp had 1,128 children, the most recent more than 5,000.

In 1971 he made a journey across Europe, in the course of which he obtained support in various quarters to build a school in a place where no one wanted to do anything, his new village of Ibillin. His supporters included Princess Beatrix in Holland, Pax Christi and the International Child's Care Organization. The building of the Mar Elias secondary school began in 1982. Today, this school has become a large complex of institutions and has 4,500 students drawn from 70 villages across the country. Elias Chacour had to fight hard to get this far, but the hardest part is now behind him. After that, conscious of the importance of education, his ambition has extended to creating the first Arab–Christian–Jewish university in Galilee.

The bishop said to him one day, 'Father Chacour, at the end of the day this college must be your life's work.' He replied, 'No. My life's work is first and foremost Jesus Christ himself. I see him in every Muslim, in every Palestinian, in every Palestinian Christian, in every Israeli Jew whom I meet. My life's work is to win their hearts, to bring a smile to their faces and to wipe away at least one of their tears. This, my Lord, is my life's work.'

That, then, is the purpose of everything that is said in this book – to seek the well-being of all, Jews as much as Palestinians. Elias Chacour is deeply convinced that both sides suffer from not being able to find love in the other, this love which they need so badly, this love which, in this present time, is their only chance of survival. He may be a Palestinian, an Arab, a Christian, an Israeli citizen, but first and foremost he is one born in the image of God. He does not pass judgement, even on actions that he cannot accept. He does everything in his power to discover the causes that lead men and women to despair and make them commit acts that are absurd, violent and murderous; for he knows that they were created to understand one another and to live and advance together in peace.

It is this message of love that he longs to pass on to his Jewish brothers in Israel and to his Muslim brothers in Palestine, not in order to convert them to his religion, but to convert them to one another in the love of God. That is why this 'other man from Galilee' speaks to us from the depth of his suffering but also from the depth of his hope.

Alain Michel

I

Two Peoples in One Land

From a distance, the Israel–Palestine conflict may seem to be something just to observe and comment on, but for me the conflict is an integral part of myself. I am Palestinian, and proud of being so. I am an Arab, my native language is Arabic and I am a Christian, but I am also an Israeli citizen. I was not born in Israel, but Israel, you might say, was born in me: I had no choice in the matter. When Israel appeared in my country it was a *fait accompli*. From my parents I inherited the conviction that the Israeli Jews are our cousins and that we are blood brothers. I also inherited the realization that those who came to Palestine before the creation of the State of Israel were survivors of the concentration camps. A 'certain devil', my father said, had tried to exterminate them – fortunately without success.

Later on I realized that these people, when they arrived in Palestine, were more than survivors of concentration camps. They had their own psychology and their own history. Because of the persecutions they had endured in Germany they claimed the right to take from the Palestinians the land which belonged to them. That is when I became aware that the creation of the State of Israel was only a partial liberation for the Jewish people – a physical liberation, but not a psychological or spiritual one. There had been created in the Jewish collective consciousness the wish to be thought of as victims by the rest of the world. It was as if an irreparable wrong had given them the right to unquestioning financial and moral support. Little by little I became aware that I, as a Palestinian, was paying the price for what others had done to my Jewish brothers, whether in Germany or elsewhere.

In the course of our efforts to build bridges with our Jewish brothers, we became conscious that this generation of Jews who have come to live in Israel is rather like the one that came out of Egypt. This one escaped the Nazis, the other the pharaohs. The one that came out of Egypt wandered in the desert for 40 years, so that the generation that had been physically liberated from slavery, but which psychologically had retained the mentality of slaves, could disappear and be replaced, before they entered the promised land, by a new generation innocent of both forms of slavery. But here, after the creation of the State of Israel, it is the same generation and often the same individuals, the survivors of the concentration camps, who have arrived in Palestine, and they still have the mentality of victims of persecution. The Jews want total liberation, cost what it may. This explains why they have always carried in themselves the sense of being victims, and why they have treated the Palestinians as if the Palestinians were an integral part of their own sufferings, often identifying them with the alien and the persecutor. For many of them, every non-Jew is a potential enemy who must be mistrusted: however much they may respect non-Jews, they can never forget to be suspicious.

To impose itself, Israel relied on military force. Its position was strengthened by the guilt complex of the West, by unconditional American support and also by the shocking lack of wisdom among the leaders of the Arab states and the total absence of a Palestinian voice. One must remember that the Palestinians themselves had only just been liberated from five centuries of Turkish slavery.

Israel has already waged several wars against the Arabs, who have always been too weak to resist. Today Israel is faced by a real problem, that of the Palestinians who have become refugees, marginalized, the 'Jews' in the Jewish state. The Palestinians have no wish that this should be their vocation. With all their strength they refuse to forget that Palestine is theirs, or to be merged into other Arab countries, which in any case (apart from Jordan) have always rejected any such solution. In Jordan, the Palestinians, who amount to 65 per cent of the population, have always made clear their determination to return home and to recover their houses, their fields and their independence. Consequently, our Jewish brothers, terrified by the idea that they might lose what they have conquered by force of arms, which they believe to be justified by a divine right of return, have reacted and continue to react with violence. They would like it to be as if the Palestinians did not exist.

Unfortunately for those who wish it were not so – or fortunately for those who wish it to be so – we do exist, and we have not the slightest intention of disappearing. We cannot accept that the only good Palestinians are dead Palestinians, just as for my part I have never accepted that a good Jew is a dead Jew. Nor have I ever accepted that a good Jew is a Jew who is labelled 'filthy Jew'. I have always been convinced that my Jewish brothers in the concentration camps were not 'filthy'. The 'filth' was the Third Reich. But, equally, I have never accepted that my own people are 'filthy' – *aravi melochlach* – or 'terrorists'. We must put an end to conflicts of this kind and be prepared to face the truth. Together, we must accept ourselves as peoples who have suffered and are still suffering. We must recall our wretched past not in order to reinforce our own identity but to make common cause with all people of good will to prevent any such persecutions, any such denials of human dignity – Jewish, Palestinian or whatever – from ever taking place again. We must find ways of convincing others, and if necessary requiring them to believe, that 'pure blood' is each and everyone's blood. The only blood that is sacred is the blood of every individual from the moment of birth. Whatever the colour, the gender, the nationality, the race or the place of birth, every individual born of woman is created in the image of God, and each one is the most beautiful, the most precious and the most sacred thing that God has created.

Who are the Palestinians?

If we listen to what the experts say about them we shall not get far. The best way to understand Palestinians is to come and see them where they live. Palestinians are village people, peaceful citizens, sociable, fond of dancing, fond of mountains, trees, fruit, flowers, the moon. They love to sing about the beauty of their country. They are highly educated, the most cultivated of all the peoples who make up the Arab world. Until about 30 years ago only seven per cent of Palestinians were illiterate, compared with sometimes more than 25 per cent in some American states. We were people who had suffered the ordeal of rejection – rejected by the Arab world, by the Jewish world, by the western world. Because of this, we came to realize that our best weapon was precisely this culture, this intellectual endowment, and that our duty was to provide the best education possible for our children.

Another thing about the Palestinians is their delight in celebrations. On a grand occasion like a marriage, it is not unusual for several hundred people to gather, Christians and Muslims together. We may have differences in our religion, but we trust one another and share almost everything.

Palestinians like to read the Bible. My mother was illiterate, she had never been to school, yet she knew the stories of the Bible, both the Old and the New Testament, by heart. She could recite passages from it faultlessly, with no lapse of memory. It was at her knee that I learnt the story of Abraham, of David, of Joseph, of Samuel, of Isaiah, of Jesus and of the apostles. It was she who told me all these stories. She did so not only out of love of the Bible, but as a way of helping me to sleep in peace. She was very devout. The Palestinian people are like that.

As we lived near the church, my parents went every Saturday evening to vespers. They went to confess their sins. I shall never forget Saturday evenings. When my parents came back they asked forgiveness for every occasion on which they had not been a good father or a good mother to the family. They said that the father of us all was God, and that this was the most important thing. We were never to forget it.

I remember also the day on which my father bought some apples. We did not have them very often because apples were expensive. That day my father gave me one. It was a beautiful apple, and I decided not to eat it in case we had an important visitor and I would be able to offer it to him. I hid it for a long time, and of course it went mouldy and I had to throw it away.

But it must not be thought that the Palestinian Christians have any monopoly of hospitality. Palestinian Muslims are also very generous. For example, one day, 40 Europeans came here into my church. They wanted to meet my parishioners and share a meal with me. It was hard enough for me to feed myself, let alone to offer hospitality to all these visitors. So, during the mass, I said to them, 'You are all westerners, you all want to have lunch. It is two o'clock. Even if you have some money to buy yourselves lunch, I am afraid there is no restaurant or grocer in our village and I have nothing to feed you with. Of course, I can offer you water, but I haven't even enough glasses for all of you. I invite you to share our way of life, which is simple, humble and modest. I invite you to think about how to accept the invitation you will receive. I am going to send you out into the streets of Ibillin. If after two hours you come back empty-handed without having found anything for lunch I will give you something to eat.'

They all went off as I told them. Three hours later they came back to take the bus. Each of them had some bread, vegetables or fruit. Four of them came back accompanied by a young Ibillin girl. One of these European ladies said to me, 'There are four of us and we were afraid of being separated from each other. But if this happened again we would certainly go separately, each of us on our own. The Christian family which welcomed us all together is an amazing family. Their generosity to us was unbelievable.' I replied that she was quite right. The Ibillin people were indeed generous; but the family that had given them such a good reception was not a Christian family but a Muslim one.

The land means a great deal to Palestinians. I learnt the value of the land from my parents. One day they bought a plot of land of 1,000 square metres. For months they worked to clear it. It was a great deal of work to get rid of all the stones. They did it with their bare hands, and the earth is saturated with their sweat and their blood. Once this was done, their very first concern was to plant a favourite tree: an olive. With their own hands they hollowed out little holes. On donkeys and on their heads they brought buckets of water for watering the field. The day they planted the olive tree was a day of celebration. There was a ritual to be followed, and then the celebration began with a banquet as if for a newborn child, so closely are we tied to the land. We were poor but we were happy. We had no computers, no television, no machines. The family was self-sufficient, and we had no doctors or psychiatrists to relieve our hurts. We died a natural death and we were all at one with each other.

Then, after 1948, when the Palestinians came to be dispersed, they settled in almost every country in the Middle East, and began to introduce their education and culture into Jordan, Egypt, Qatar, Kuwait, Iraq. This mission of the Palestinian people involved extreme suffering. To give an example: one of my cousins lives in Lebanon, his wife lives in Athens. As for their children, one lives in Israel, the other in the USA. They have had to live apart for more than 40 years. Yet they harbour no hatred and if one asks how that is possible, the answer is that hatred does not interest them. Their only wish is to return home, to rebuild their houses, to recover their roots and enjoy the respect of others.

The Palestinians are what they are because of all the conquests they have been subjected to, and because of having had to mingle with all their occupiers. Near Ibillin, for example, there is a town called Tamra. At Tamra, unlike Ibillin, the inhabitants are Muslims: they are tall, they have blue eyes and fair hair. You would think they were westerners. When he was planning to attack Ako, Napoleon established his headquarters at Tamra. He has been gone a long time, but he left something behind him at Tamra. The Muslims were originally Christians who later converted to Islam. These Christians were the descendants of the first Christian community; and the first Christian community after Jesus Christ was Jewish. So one of my fingers may be Jewish, the second Greek, the third Roman, the fourth perhaps Byzantine. No one can prove it to be otherwise. No one has the right to say to me, 'I have lived here for 2,000 years. You weren't here then, so go away.' I was here before that. I have always been here. I have as much right to the land as anyone else, perhaps even more.

The Jews, of course, have also lived in dispersion in Palestine. There were Jewish minorities in Meiron, in Safed, in Tiberias, in Jerusalem. For several centuries they were highly prosperous in Damascus and Beirut, and also in Morocco. Indeed, Morocco has been a kind of oasis for the Jewish people since time immemorial. Up to the end of the 1950s the Jews also lived peacefully in Iraq. According to the account of a distinguished Jew, a Jewish movement, which shall be nameless, placed bombs in Iraqi synagogues to convince the Jews there that they should come to the Holy Land – which they did. But it never occurred to the Palestinians to persecute them.

When, at the beginning of the twentieth century, the Zionist movement began to send Jews to Palestine, the Palestinians welcomed them with open arms. But what happened to the Palestinians then is like what happened to the native Americans when the Spanish colonizers arrived. Even so, it never occurred to us to persecute the Jews who lived among us. We are not the Jews' enemies. We want to be their friends.

The expulsion

What happened in 1948 was worse than anything that is happening today. Four hundred and sixty Palestinian towns and villages were completely destroyed. Hundreds of thousands of Palestinians were expelled from their homes. I was one of them. My home was in Bar-am; and I can remember perfectly the Jews whom we welcomed into our houses when they arrived after leaving the concentration camps. We killed the fatted calf for them, as my father used to do to celebrate Easter. He said to us, 'Our Jewish brothers who have come to us are like people raised from the dead. They have escaped Hitler's hell, we must welcome them.' We offered them our beds. As a child I slept on the roof to give them room. And yet, ten days later, they gave orders to all heads of families to lock their houses, give the key to an officer and go away for two weeks. 'Take nothing with you, other than your wives and children. You will be back in two weeks. Here is your certificate, a written undertaking that you will be able to return without difficulty in two weeks' time.' It was a time of war, of violence and of fear, but, being assured we could return, and relying on the word of the soldiers whom we had welcomed, we left. I remember it well. It was evening. I had taken a blanket with me and we left for the 'two weeks'. Fifty-four years later the two weeks are still not up, we have never returned. Despite a judgement of the Supreme Court of Israel in our favour, our village was destroyed on 24 December 1951, Christmas Eve.

My father always said to us, 'Don't forget to return to Bar-am. It is our village. That is where you will find your roots. But never use violence, even if it has been used against you.'

The one thing my father wanted was to rebuild our family house, the house of our ancestors, and to die there. Ten years ago he died in Haifa. There was no possibility for him to return to Bar-am alive, but we buried him in the cemetery there. What we wish for ourselves is to return there *before* we die, so that we can say to the Jews, 'You have done us great injury, but today let us share our respective sufferings. Let us look to a better future together.'

The dream of every one of the inhabitants of Bar-am, our dearest dream, is always that of being able to return home. In July 2001 I received a visit from my nephew, who had lived in America for 23 years. He married an American and has five daughters and a son, Michael, who was then seven. When I asked Michael, 'Where do you come from?', he replied, 'From Bar-am.' I said to him, 'But no, you are from Indiana.' He replied, 'No, Indiana is my temporary home. It is not my country. My country is Bar-am' – and he is a child only seven years old! The Jews have to forgive us for having a memory as good as theirs! We are like the exiles in Babylon, we live, we build houses, we do business, we have children – and yet we plead with tears to return to our 'Zion': Palestine.

I once had the honour of welcoming Mr Shimon Peres to the school. This visit is connected with a story I shall tell later about James Baker, then the American Secretary of State. Mr Peres wanted to come and give a lecture for us on peace. Over a cup of coffee I reminded him that I am a native of Bar-am and that the inhabitants of that village were still waiting to return. There were about 70 distinguished guests present. He said to me, 'But, Father Chacour, look at your school! You have built a veritable palace here! It's amazing! It's better than our Jewish schools! And now you have been here 50 years! You left

Bar-am when you were eight. After 50 years, don't you think it is time to forget Bar-am?' I looked at him and answered, 'Mr Peres, forgive me if what I am going to say is a bit cheeky. But haven't you got memories too? You left Palestine 2,000 years ago and you have come back to make our lives hell. Tell me, Mr Peres, when are you going to forget that Palestine is your country?' He said to me, 'Please excuse me, I deserved that reply.'

Today, we are exiles in our own country. We are refugees, refugees from the heart of Israel, refugees *in* the heart of Israel. Meanwhile our village has been destroyed and is a heap of ruins, our fields have been stripped and become wild woodland. One way of putting it is to say that Israel is pregnant, and its embryo is Palestine. Some mothers take care of themselves and the child is born healthy. Some mothers maltreat the child while it is still in the womb and it is born handicapped, in which case it may grow to be a very heavy burden for its mother, a cross for her to bear. Some mothers even kill their child, and by doing so incur their own death. We want the embryo to come to birth and Israel to be the mother who allows it to be born, to grow and to reach adulthood. In our society abortion is a crime. We will not allow Israel to become a criminal. Israel has no right to abort Palestine and destroy itself.

The power of memories

If you want to shake hands, this does not mean that you must forget. It is essential to remember the past and all its horrors. But that is what memory is about: one can't change or control the past. One must not get stuck in it and so waste one's time in a past that can be neither controlled nor changed. But equally, one must not use it to justify acts like those that were committed in the past. If, in the past, I have been persecuted, if again and again I have heard the words 'filthy Arab', 'Palestinian terrorist', 'I am going to do to you what Hitler did to us', I have to remember it, but not in order to reproduce it now, but in order to ally myself with my Jewish brother to prevent it happening again.

Some say that memory is the past preserved in the present. We cannot do anything about it. Yet to forget the past would be to neglect and deny what one has lived through, it would be to destroy our memory of reality. Moreover, we can be in control of the present, and this can be so thanks to common action on the part of enemies who are both suffering, and thanks also to a common will to get together to build the foundations of a better future. What sort of future do we want to give to Jewish children born in Israel and to Palestinian children born in refugee camps? We surely should not accept a *status quo* that was created by force and violence. We should begin to change it from today, so as to bring to birth a kind of distributive justice both for those who have occupied the land at the point of a bayonet and for those who, having no lobby in America, have never known what went on in the western world with regard to the Jews. The Palestinians knew nothing of all the conspiracies that were being hatched, but they were the victims of them. All of that demands reparation. Without it, Israel can become ten times stronger but will never enjoy peace and security. Together, Israeli Jews and Palestinians, we should join hands in a gigantic common effort to declare once and for all that 'might is not right'. Otherwise we must be on our guard, all of us. A 'strong one in our midst', capable of destroying our pride, our Twin Towers, could secretly destroy the very heart of our means of defence, even if we had a Pentagon more powerful and more heavily protected than the Pentagon in the United States. The nightmare of a biological or chemical war has no frontiers, and is alas by no means impossible.

Our Jewish brothers – what did they do at Masada against the injustice of the Romans? What did they do near Tiberias, at Mount Arabel? Did they not resist slavery to the point of death? What did they do in the Second World War? Did they not use every possible means of resistance at Auschwitz and at Teretsin? They had good reason to do so. So it is not for them to become tyrants and executioners in their turn. I want to make an appeal to all our brothers, to all human beings, and in particular to all Jewish and Muslim fundamentalists and fanatics: 'Stop killing! Stop killing in the name of religion!' The people responsible for this evil are religious people. It is as if human beings are having a race with God and God has to run after them to try to catch them up. Sometimes he does catch them up, sometimes he fails to – but that is because he has given us free will. Humans may think they are killing for God – but God does not kill! It is impossible to justify war or injustice by invoking God.

I invite all my Jewish brothers, especially the Israeli television people when they give interviews or hold meetings, not to forget the first two questions which their Creator put to them. The first was, 'Man, where are you?' He was hiding because he had done wrong. The second was, 'Where is your brother? What have you done with your brother?' When my Jewish brother asks me, 'What did you, you people of the West and elsewhere, what did you do about your brother during the Second World War?', I can respond by asking in my turn, 'My

Jewish brother, what are you doing about your Palestinian brother?' He may reply, 'Am I your keeper?'; but in that case I will say to him, 'Yes, you are my keeper, for I shall never be happy without you, and you too will never be happy without me.'

The Jews of Israel and the State of Israel may yet survive if they take the Palestinians by the hand and say, 'We have suffered all these atrocities, we regret having made you suffer because of our suffering, can we not move forward together? Let us acknowledge the atrocities of the past, whether they were in Europe or in Palestine, but let us choose a better future for our children.' We must be ruthless in the face of all forms of apartheid, whether that of the Third Reich, of extremist Zionism or of Muslim fundamentalism. All human beings deserve our compassion and our forgiveness if we are to look forward to a better future. That is how I see the future of Israel. The Jewish people must not make the mistake of thinking that every non-Jew is a potential enemy. To do so would be to trample on human rights, which is something we cannot accept. We love the Jews, we think of them as our brothers. And the same goes for the people of Gaza and the West Bank. Our Jewish brothers seem to have forgotten the importance of dignity and pride, even though they have retained them for themselves. Israel has a life before it, and I pray for that. But Israel must not go on behaving like a master among slaves. We cannot accept being treated like slaves.

Women could play an important part in the creation of peace in Israel. It is true that when Golda Meir was Prime Minister she was the very opposite of a key to peace. Nevertheless, I take the view that if there were more women involved in the negotiations there would very likely be more chance of reaching an understanding. Israel may be a modern and democratic state but in fact it is governed indirectly by the religious parties, and these do not recognize the rights of women. Indeed, if they were able to exclude women from all public services they would do so without hesitation. According to the Talmud the testimony of a man is worth that of two women. There is a real conflict between rabbinic law and civil law in Israel. On the one side are Jewish lay people, who have no desire for a rigid theocracy, and on the other are the religious parties, which are becoming stronger all the time. These two groups are profoundly opposed to each other. One explanation for this may be the re-appearance of poverty, linked to a growth in unemployment.

But to come back to the role of women: there already exist Palestinian movements for peace within Israel and an on-going dialogue between Jewish and Arab women. One cannot expect the same to be true on the West Bank, for there the situation is different. But even if Israeli Arab women take part in social and political life, their emancipation is only beginning. We need time, we are still far from our objective. We cannot expect all the women of the West Bank and Gaza to be Hanan Ashrawis![1]

Palestinians are a generous people. They are used to the invasions of foreign powers, they are used to occupation. The Romans were there for centuries. So were the Ottomans. But none of our conquerors were able to survive without treating us equitably. We do not want to be avenged of our present persecutions, but we cannot accept our present status of second-

---

1 Hanan Ashrawi was formerly Minister of Higher Education in Arafat's cabinet. She is quite open in denouncing the undemocratic procedures of the Palestinian Authority.

class citizens. I wish to be a first-class Israeli citizen, with the same status as a Jew coming from Russia, America or Africa. None of these can claim more rights over Palestine than I, a Palestinian. We are ready to share, but not to be stripped of everything. That may happen elsewhere, but it cannot happen in Palestine.

If there is to be peace, it is imperative that Israel does certain things – and I am talking about Israel specifically, not Jews in general. First, it must acknowledge that we who are refugees have been paying for what others have done to the Jews. Second, it must recognize that it has nothing to *give* to the Palestinians: we do not want condescension, we do not want charity. It must simply give back what it has taken from us by force and withdraw from the occupied territories. Finally, Israeli Jews must accept the idea that the Palestinians are potential friends and not enemies. They must get rid of their conviction, which has grown upon them in the course of their history, that every non-Jew is a potential enemy. They must come to terms with this destructive mentality which they have inherited from past centuries, a mentality of 'tolerate but be on your guard'.

2

Terrorism: 'For me, dying is gain . . .'

Fear in Israel

Since the second Intifada, the Israelis have been manifesting acute anxiety. They are convinced that the Palestinians have no other desire than to see them be thrown into the sea. It has become a real obsession, almost a phobia; and it is an idea that the Jews have felt the need to spread in order to gain still more sympathy from the West. The idea came from a man who lived on Lake Como in Italy. In 1956, when the Palestinians were living in fear of Israel, he came to the Ambassador Hotel in Jerusalem and said to them, 'But why are you afraid? Don't worry, we shall throw them all into the sea.' Three days later this gentleman went away, and later on was found dead in a night-club. He had drunk too much. After that, the Zionist movement took over the phrase and spread it round the world; and it became an idea that has done more harm to the Palestinians than to the Jews. For it expresses the exact opposite of what Palestinians really want. What we want is to live with the Jews of Israel in peace, sharing the land with mutual respect.

The Israelis have also become afraid because of what they have inflicted on the Palestinians; for they cannot forget that Palestine is Palestinian and that they are living on Palestinian land. And they are frightened – which is curious, because they are armed to the teeth, whereas we, who are completely without any such protection and are being killed every day, have no fear at all. They may have the military power, they may live in houses protected by barbed wire and police dogs, but they do not have the security of right on their side; for might is *not* always right, despite Lafontaine's fable of *The Fox and the Lamb*.

Another thing that disturbs the Jews is that we are still free to have children, thousands of children. It is hardly possible to castrate the Palestinians, but it is certainly possible to see that children are brought up with a commitment to peace, justice and the sociable mingling of races. Education could be an antidote to fear; but the habitual infringement of human rights produces only bitterness and the desire for revenge. These are what cause violence and terrorism.

Today the Jews have yet another fear – a fear that is beginning to be felt throughout the West. They fear a religion that we know little about: Islam. We are beginning to realize that Islam is not an Arab movement: the Arabs are a minority in the world's Muslim population, and the West too is beginning to feel threatened. But here in Israel, in this small fraction of the West, we are not afraid of Islam. On the contrary, what we are afraid of is not Islam, but any form of fundamentalism, be it Muslim, Christian or Jewish.

Of course, we must not generalize. The Jews in general are not the same as the Israeli government. As people, we have a great deal in common. At Christmas we once organized a big dinner at the college, and all my Jewish brothers were present. Many others had telephoned me to wish me a Happy Christmas. In the same way, for Hanukka, the festival of light, I do not hesitate to light candles. It is my light as well! Why should the Jews keep to themselves festivals that are equally mine? The same goes for Muslims: *Allah aqbar* (God is great) is also a Christian prayer! We must cherish what we have in common not only for the sake of mutual respect but also for mutual flourishing. But at the same time, one has to hold individuals responsible. I am thinking particularly of the soldiers who burn houses, kill people, pursue human beings as if they were brute beasts and hide behind state authority so that they can commit these disgraceful crimes with impunity. If we are to allow people to hide behind state authority in Israel and say that the soldiers and the army are not responsible for what they do, how can we say to the Germans that the guards at Auschwitz were guilty? Surely their duty was to rebel and refuse to obey laws that were patently unjust?

The causes of terrorism

The young people here have come to believe that they have lost everything, and this has opened a door to terrorism, a terrorism reinforced by religious principles. If the Palestinians have nothing left to protect, no houses, no territory, no independence, not even their own dignity, then nothing will stop the terrorists and Israel will always be afraid.

For dignity matters. I am reminded of a rather sad story. When electricity was installed in the refugee camps, very few people had enough money to buy a television set. Those who had one put on airs and felt superior to the others. Then a number of people went to great lengths to fix an aerial on their little shack so that no one could say, 'You are poor, you can't afford a television set.' By doing that, they wanted to protect their dignity, because that was all that was left to them. My

Jewish brothers have to understand this: dignity is as important to my Palestinian brothers and sisters as life itself.

Ever since the horrible attack on the United States, 9/11, I have noticed that the tone has become revengeful and violent. I have not yet heard a single word of forgiveness or of reconciliation. There has not been a single initiative, a single response that could have restored dignity to the poor. When you get a poor wretch into a corner to kill him, before he dies he will stamp his foot and say, 'To hell with this life!' Isn't that what is happening to young Palestinians? How often have they been imprisoned, beaten, humiliated? They would rather die bravely than live like cowards. It is time we should wake up to all these horrors: they simply breed more of the same.

I can well understand that when there are suicide attacks in Israel the mothers, the children, indeed everyone, is frightened when they go out for a walk or go shopping in the supermarket. To get rid of this fear, Israel has to give the Palestinians back their confidence, saying to them, 'We have taken your country. We are giving back 10 per cent of it, or 20 per cent. Come now, we are ready to live with you.' But it must stop saying, 'Go away wherever you want. Go and live with other Arabs.' When there is an attack, we must no longer hear and see on television, 'Death to the Arabs'. Terrorism is as much Jewish as Palestinian. To curb it, we have to break the vicious circle of violence.

It is true that in some parts of the occupied territories children are taught to hate the Jews. But what can be expected of people who have been forced to live in refugee camps that are often not very different from concentration camps? This was certainly the case in Tel Azzatar, in Sabra and Chatila, and during 'black September' in Jordan. You can't ask Palestinians to be angels when they are living in hell. In Jericho the population has been virtually in prison since 2001: they cannot leave or enter because of the trenches or check-points that surround their town. In Hebron 120,000 Arabs are deprived of their liberty in order to guarantee the security of 300 fanatical colonists. What do you think the parents of Israeli Jewish children say in the colonies on the West Bank or in Israel when they are living on land confiscated from the Palestinians? And what does a Palestinian family that was once the proprietor of this land say to its children? I imagine that the Jews say, 'This is our land, it belonged to us 2,000 years ago.' For their part, Palestinians have to say, 'It is our land, we live here, and the Jews have driven us out and taken our place.' And what are Palestinian parents to say to their children when they cannot send them to school, or when bombs are destroying their houses and bullets are killing their menfolk? What are they to say to their children when they ask where these bombs and bullets come from? Of course they reply, 'It is all the fault of the Jews.' Of course they generalize, and that is how hatred takes over.

The Palestinians cannot tell lies to their children. 'Mummy, why are we living in a refugee camp?' 'Because the Jews took our village.' 'Mummy, why don't we have as much freedom as the Jewish children?' 'Because we are living under occupation, and the Jews are the occupiers.'

I am afraid that the education of Jewish children with regard to the Palestinians is no better than that of Palestinian children with regard to the Jews. Television has a destructive influence, in the sense that all Arabs are lumped together as 'the enemy', as 'terrorists'. It is an influence that corrupts the hearts of the children. Both sides must make an effort to counter this indoctrination by the media.

Why is it forbidden to talk about Palestine in Israel? What are we to say to the children? That we were born out of the clouds? Palestinian teachers have to begin their lessons by saying to the children, 'We would very much like to teach you the history of Palestine, but Israel forbids us to speak of Palestine. That is why we cannot teach you its history.' By doing this Israel is fostering terrorism. Those who have nothing because someone has confiscated all they possess have no hesitation in committing suicide and involving in their death those who have taken everything from them.

So what is a terrorist? Is it someone who throws a bomb into a crowd, or is it someone who throws someone else into despair to the point where that person has nothing to do but throw a bomb in return? Simple definitions will not help us. The real questions lie deeper.

Where is God in all this?

When God created us, he willed us to be free. There is no greater proof of God's divinity than the fact that he gave us free will. But this free will of ours is ambivalent: when we act, we do not always know how to choose the good. Those who choose to commit suicide, subjecting innocent people to certain death, have forfeited their God-given freedom. They have become slaves to their despair.

I have always been convinced that God does not kill: he never has and never will. Think of Joshua, for example, when he entered the Promised Land. It did not belong to the Jews; but what country could seem more beautiful than Jericho to people who had been wandering for 40 years in the desert? The rich abundance of Jericho was a temptation. So Joshua massacred all its inhabitants, sparing only Rahab the prostitute. Doing so, he did evil in the name of God. The crime he committed was not just to have massacred an entire town, it was to have killed in the name of God.

Today, it is Christ who is needed – the Christ who, instead of taking vengeance, hangs on the cross and calls on God saying, 'Father, forgive them for they know not what they do', a Christ who says to us, 'Love your enemies, bless those who insult you.' Don't imagine I find this easier than anyone else does. I am not in the least inclined to love my enemies and bless those who insult me, especially when they have destroyed my father's house in Bar-am.

That reminds me that in my office there is a splendid mirror that was given me by a friend in New Mexico. He suggested I wrote beneath the mirror the words, 'Come and see the most beautiful thing that God has created.' Every person who looks in this mirror is indeed a creature, the finest of God's creations. Every time one sees oneself there, one must remember these two questions, which God puts to us: 'Man, where are you?', and 'Man, where is your brother?' The man hid himself because he had done wrong; but I, despite the wrong I have suffered, am my brother's keeper. If not, I do wrong too.

There are things which God allows to happen that we cannot explain. One can only try to learn from the past. How often have human beings rebelled against their Creator? How often have they said no to God? When they depart from the source of their life, which is God, and become embroiled with sin and corruption, they die. It makes no difference what the situation is: the moment one chooses evil instead of heeding God, it become insoluble. Why did God allow 3,000 families to be broken for ever by the events of September 11th? There is no explanation: it is the cost of human free will used for an evil purpose.

The Third World knew what globalization was going to do to them. There have been demonstrations at Seattle to protest against the abuses that have been its result. In the course of one of these demonstrations in Italy a person was killed. But none of that has been enough for a change of heart. So what is needed so that we may be brought to see evil? Do six million Jews have to be killed so that we can see the evil that was incarnated in Hitler? Do a million and a half Armenians have to be killed so that we can see the evil rooted in the Ottoman ideology? Do the same number of Palestinians have to be killed so that we can see the evil rooted in a pernicious interpretation of Zionism, one that does as much harm to the Jews as it does to the Palestinians? What are we to say about what happened in Cambodia? I went myself to Cambodia with an international delegation. I saw where hundreds of men and women had been buried alive after having worked for weeks in the paddy fields. Those who had already succumbed had been left where they were to fertilize the ground. The others had been thrown into a ditch and buried with earth. One could still smell the appalling stench when I arrived at the spot. How can such atrocities be explained?

Perhaps God gives the explanation. But where is God? How can he allow all this to happen? I do not know, no one knows. Where was God when Cain killed Abel? The question I ask myself is a different one. How is it possible for us to be so cruel, to ignore the source of our existence, the divine source of love, compassion and kindness? Whether we were Palestinian, French or American, our mothers carried us for nine months before we were born. But that does not mean that it is our destiny to be our mothers' property for ever. As a believer, I am destined for rebirth to eternal life, and it is God's will that it should be for me to decide what the quality of that eternal life will be. For nothing in the world would I change my faith in Jesus Christ – however much politicians may think he was mad and soldiers may think he was ineffective.

The words of Christ on the cross mean that it is we ourselves, not God the Father, who will pass judgement on us. This judgement will not depend on the number of times we have been to church, or the number of times we have stood up for our religion, or on our knowledge of one doctrine or another. It will depend on some very simple facts. I was hungry and you refused me food. I was a prisoner and you refused to set me free. I was sick and you refused to support me, I was naked and you refused to give me something to wear. It all depends on what we have or have not done. It is not enough just not to do evil, one has also to do good. The rich fellow who gave banquets for his friends was not a robber or a tyrant, but at the last judgement he went down to hell, not because he had become too fat but because he had chosen to be blind and had not tried to do good. He had not helped Lazarus, whose sores were licked by the dogs to give him relief. Even the dogs were more charitable than he was.

Jesus Christ says to me: 'Yes, you must love your neighbour, but to love him you have first to get to know him.' Very often Jesus disturbs me, amazes me and troubles me. Jesus is a disturber of conscience. He stops one sleeping peacefully, he stops one living as if there was nothing to do but indulge one's egoism. I do not believe he was a disembodied spirit come down from heaven. His blood was not special divine blood, but the

25

blood of a woman, one of our women who lived in Nazareth. He experienced an occupation just as our children experience it today in the refugee camps. He had the same mentality. He was a troublemaker. His friends – the first of them was the Samaritan woman – were 'the rabble', 'terrorists' who were stabbing the Romans. He said, 'Before you go off to war, take thought and make peace first.' That is why I do not believe there is such a thing as a *just* war. There is only war, and both sides are losers. All too often we Christians have exploited our Master, simply making him a tool for promoting our fantasies. Today, we are as far from Christ as the earth is from the moon.

3

Jews and Palestinians in the Holy Land

In October 2000 one of my students was killed by the Israeli army. He was on his way home, and he was the first to get out of the bus. He was also the first to be captured, and he was killed in cold blood. He was one of my most brilliant students, 17 years old, named Assil Assli. There is a site on the internet devoted to him, containing testimonies to the life of this young person. He was a member of a group called 'Seeds of Peace', which consisted of young people, Jews and Palestinians, from the West Bank, Israel and Egypt. They had elected him their leader and he was the spokesman for peace between Israeli Jewish and Palestinian children. We had sent them to Washington, where they had met Hillary Clinton as well as several senators and members of Congress to plead for the establishment of peace between our two nations. This is the young person who was killed. I conducted his funeral myself along with 30,000 Muslims. I was the only Christian there among the teachers.

The Israelis would not admit that he had been killed in cold blood: he was accused of throwing stones at a soldier. Barak had given the army carte blanche, including the right to shoot Israeli citizens. On this occasion 13 people were killed, Assil

Assli among them. In two days 300 were wounded. When the Israeli police had to give evidence before the Supreme Court on the cause of death of this boy, they replied, 'The second cassette recording witnesses' statements has not been transcribed yet, let us go on to the third.' In this way the statements that proved their responsibility for it were suppressed.

How should we Palestinians react to such things? Since we will never be a military power, we have had to ask ourselves whether we ought to adopt an attitude of total non-violence, following the example of Gandhi. We have thought a great deal about this. But, first of all, it is important to realize that the environment in which Gandhi evolved was quite different from ours. Palestinians like to compare themselves with David confronted by Goliath. The fact that our enemy has more powerful weapons does not frighten us in any way. Goliath imagined he was invincible but was laid out by a mere pebble. What is needed for victory today is not military power but legitimacy and perseverance in the application of law. Israel may have military might, but it is we who have right on our side. Israel convinced the rest of the world that it needed a buffer zone: South Lebanon, the West Bank and the Jordan. In 1990 this zone disappeared. Iraqi missiles arrived from more than 1,000 kilometres away. Israel could not stop them, nor could American missiles.

Today there is no such thing as a buffer zone. If Israel wants to have security it has two options: either to win the friendship of the Palestinians, and so of the entire Arab world – which is not very difficult – or else to exterminate all Palestinians as well as the rest of the Arab world – which is absurd. There is nothing noble about suicide and murder. If anything is noble, it is protecting oneself and others. And that is my wish for

Israel: that it may defend its existence – so long as Israel grants me a place within the Israeli state and that I can become a full citizen. Even a mad prime minister would not dare to order the army to fire on its own citizens, to fire on me, one citizen among the rest who has never wished Israel any harm. Our demand is simply for the application of the same justice for all, the creation of a state with the same laws for all and a status for us as full citizens at its heart.

Take the case of my village Bar-am, which is typical. We possessed 12,500 hectares of land. The kibbutzim around us confiscated about 5,000, the rest was abandoned as a kind of no man's land. We wrote to several successive Israeli governments and to various other people. We were not trying to claim back the land that the kibbutzim had appropriated, but only the land that had been abandoned. After 53 years we were finally given permission to return. Out of the 12,500 hectares that had been confiscated we were given the right to repossess 600. We had to sign a document to the effect that we were giving up our claim to the rest. We thanked the government for having recognized our right of return and also for the 600 hectares that were to be given back, but we refused to go back ourselves unless we could open negotiations about the rest of the land we were entitled to. This was refused. This is just one example of many. A state can hardly survive on the basis of such injustice.

I do not feel any hatred towards the Jews. What would that mean? To wish they were dead is something that I would never do. On the other hand, to be revolted by what they do – yes indeed. I am certainly revolted by their obstinate refusal to admit that I have a right to return to my own village of Bar-am. This I find unacceptable. Indeed, I did not hesitate to say to Golda Meir in 1973 that the people of Bar-am had the right to return to their village, they had the right to return home. I said to her that she was playing the part of Jezebel, the wife of the King of Israel, who killed Naboth in order to acquire his land and join it to that of the King. I told her that no matter how much force and power she had, if she did this she would kill justice in Israel. I sense that what they are doing to the Palestinians is a kind of self-destruction, as if they were trying to create their own devil – hence the sufferings of the Palestinians, which I find it impossible to accept.

In all that is happening at the moment in Israel, the Israeli government is showing that it is determined to humiliate others who are unarmed and have no military resources to defend themselves. One could almost say that Mr Sharon delighted in inflicting this humiliation on others, a gratuitous humiliation that served no purpose. The Palestinians ought to have written a letter of thanks to Mr Sharon for having forbidden Mr Arafat from going to Bethlehem at Christmas 2001. By this refusal he revealed to world opinion the political and military arrogance of one who despised all human, religious and spiritual values. In my view, we needed an Israeli prime minister who would not just have allowed Mr Arafat to go to Bethlehem on his own, but instead would have picked him up in his car on the way. Then they would have gone together to sing a song of peace, mutual respect and the glory of God. That single gesture would have solved the Israeli–Palestinian question. But one could hardly have expected Mr Sharon to take a peace initiative as unbelievable, as unexpected and as spontaneous as this. Had he done so, he would have been elected by the entire world as the Man of the Year, 2002.

Unfortunately, in a kind of way, Mr Sharon did a notable service to Mr Arafat and the Palestinians by humiliating them so publicly. By doing so, he filled people with hatred for the Jews; he created a new threat, a new danger for himself. Mr Sharon did not understand that it was not enough to be powerful, one must also have wisdom. Wisdom, it seems, was the particular gift of Solomon. But Solomon is dead. At the present time there is no Solomon in Israel.

Within the last 50 years one person did take a truly courageous initiative: I mean Anwar Saddat. In 1979, when Israel occupied Sinai and violence was increasing, Saddat went to Israel and spoke to the Israelis in these terms: 'I have come among you, and here, in your Parliament, I want to speak to you.' It was a powerful initiative, even a prophetic one. If only today we could have an Israeli leader who, like General de Gaulle for the French, could say to the Israeli Jews and the Palestinians, 'I understand you all. The time for colonies is over. It is time to build a country for the Palestinians and the Jews together. It is time to work for peace, for the security of all and for equal justice.'

So far as reprisals by the Arab nations are concerned, I thought and hoped that Mr Arafat would be more sensible than Mr Sharon. At least he was wiser, more moderate, and closer to some kind of reconciliation. Another leader might have taken his cue from Mr Sharon, and not hesitated to take his army to certain death in Israel and to do all he could to create mayhem – even though to commit a diabolical action in retaliation for being humiliated is hardly meritorious. But fortunately Mr Arafat acted decently: he was well aware of his own humiliation, and of the arrogance of the Israeli army. He said straight out that this was an obstacle to the peace process. What he said – and it is very evocative – was simply this: 'I was going to Bethlehem to pray to the Prince of peace.' A Muslim who says,

'I am going to pray to the Prince of peace to bring us peace and justice' teaches us all a lesson. Even the leaders of Christian states do not do as much. I think that the idea of Mr Arafat in his headgear, seated in the Church of St Catherine on Christmas Eve, was something more eloquent than anything else around at the time. Even China protested against the refusal and the insult that Mr Sharon had offered to the person with whom he had to negotiate peace in the Middle East. The truth is that even if Mr Arafat had come to kneel in front of Mr Sharon, Mr Sharon would never have agreed to talk about peace. The question did not interest him, it had never interested him. When Mr Peres had the almost unimaginable idea of handing back 42 per cent of their land to the Palestinians, he was met by a categorical no from Mr Sharon. The Palestinians were not even allowed to put in a word. Can they be blamed, then, for losing hope? But when one loses hope, the consequences for both sides are disastrous.

I pray constantly that the State of Israel may have a leader who has the charisma and the gifts needed to plan for 20 years in the future instead of living 20 years in the past. I pray that the Palestinians may not need a holocaust of two or three million dead before the world wakes up and becomes aware of the realities of Israel–Palestine. The wretched conditions in which Palestinians live in the refugee camps cannot go on. It is something that has got to stop. I pray that the world may come to realize that the Palestinians are not intruders, that they have an absolute right to live in this land, and that their roots are here, in Israel. I pray that the international community may be vigilant enough to prevent a new crime being committed against a whole nation.

The flight of Christians

The Christians are leaving because they want their children to be brought up in peace, security and tranquillity. Most of them left in 1948 and it was only a minority who remained. The Christians living in the Holy Land make up about 25 per cent of Palestinian Christians worldwide. The rest are in refugee camps, in exile or in what is called the diaspora – voluntary exile. All their land has been confiscated by Israel for building settlements: Beit Jala, Guilo, Beit Saour were Christian properties. As for the question whether it would suit the Jews for the Christians to leave, it is better not to ask. We Christians can do more harm to the Jews than all the Muslims in the world put together: Muslims are marginalized and discredited in the West, whereas a Christian, who speaks the language of European Christians, can speak out with some chance of being heard.

It is also true, I believe, that the Palestinian Christians are having to pay the penalty that many of the Jews believe western Christians should pay. Contrary to what is widely believed in the West, the Muslims in Nazareth, and the Muslim world in general, have no desire to see the Palestinian Christians leave Israel. Besides, their children are in our schools: 65 per cent of my students are Muslims, and it is the same in all the schools in Nazareth. There is not a single Muslim school there, they are all Christian.

The Christians of the West feel a certain alarm with regard to Muslims. They have the idea that Islam wants to drive them out of the East. But it does not feel like that in Israel. If the Christians are leaving, it is not because of Islam. We have lived with Islam since the time of the Prophet. The disciples of

Muhammad would have been killed if the Christians had not been there to protect them. There was a time when Muslims were invited to come and pray in churches. Islam is no enemy to Christians, at least in the East. It has become the enemy of the Christian West because it threatens the western economy. The fact is that the West has always refused to get to know Islam – until 9/11, when everyone suddenly became interested. In Palestine it is different, for we live together, we have suffered together and we continue to suffer together. For myself, I am invited more frequently to Muslim weddings than to Christian ones. We have certainly had problems, but these have never had anything to do with race or religion. When we had difficulties, we supported each other. It has never occurred to the Muslims to want to drive us out. We are an integral part of their environment, of their very way of life.

The reasons why Christians feel forced to emigrate are quite different. They cannot find work and they cannot educate their children as they would wish: the atmosphere has become too oppressive. In 1948 there were 40,000 Christians in Jerusalem. If they had stayed, there would be a quarter of a million today. But there are only 6,000 left. The truth is that they were deported when the State of Israel came into existence – that was true of the Christian community in Safed, in Tiberias, in my village of Bar-am and in the village of Ikrit. Today, all that is taken for granted. No one finds it extraordinary. It was not Islam that drove out the Christians from Damun, from Jaffa, from Haifa, from Latrun. It was the creation of a political entity that was hostile to everything foreign to it.

A linked destiny

I remember the day when there was a horrifying bomb attack in Tel Aviv. A Palestinian suicide bomber had blown himself up at the bus station in retaliation for the massacre in the Hebron mosque committed by Baruch Goldstein, the Nazi Jew who had killed some Muslims while they were at prayer. That day 20 Jews were killed and 80 were wounded. My students – at that time there were 350 of them – had wanted to do something to protest against the massacre of Palestinians at Hebron. We wrote to the Minister of the Interior and the Minister of Education, saying how shocked we were by such terrorist acts that were unworthy of Jews who still had memories of the Holocaust. But then, in the face of the bomb attack in Tel Aviv, we got together letters of solidarity and sympathy intended for the Jewish families. My students were saying to me, 'This is not enough.' And one of them said, 'I am ready to give my blood for those who have been taken to hospital.' Another said he too was ready to do the same. As a priest, I could not forbid them, and I was glad to hear them say it. I immediately telephoned the Rambam Hospital in Haifa. When I told them that I had some students who wanted to give blood, they hesitated but finally believed me. Sure enough, next day at eight in the morning there were several hospital vehicles in front of the school. I was afraid that no more than five or six students would give their blood, which would have made it a farce. But out of 350 students, 300 did so. I shall always remember that when it was my turn, there were lying next to me a Druze teacher, a Jew, and an American volunteer, and there we were side by side giving blood for our well-beloved brothers.

'We don't agree with what you are doing, but we will never agree to put an end to your lives' – that was the message that we hoped this gesture would convey. That day I said on Israeli television, 'Today I can hope to return, for there is now Palestinian blood flowing in Jewish veins. It is a way of saving a life that might have been extinguished. And we are not willing it should be extinguished. We are ready to give up our own lives so that others should live. Today it is for the Jews; but the same goes for others, and it goes, of course, for our Palestinian brothers and sisters.'

Solidarity can be shown in both directions. I know that the Jews are capable of similar initiatives and can show solidarity with the Palestinian people. Some time ago seven Reformed Rabbis, modernizing and by no means fanatical, arrived in my office. They wanted to talk to me about working together for peace. I said to them, 'I have no wish to talk about peace just now. Far from it: my concern at this moment is to get several tons of food to Beit Jala where people are dying of hunger.' They replied, 'But what is preventing you? There is no law against it.' I said to them, 'No, but it costs a lot of money. We need two lorries and each one costs $700. If you rabbis really want peace, give me the money!' Immediately, $1,400 were laid on the table. Then I said to them, 'Very well, but that is not enough. I do not know how to get these two lorries filled with foodstuffs across the frontier.' They replied, 'But there isn't a frontier.' To which I replied, 'On the contrary, there are several metres of no man's land, and if we cross it the army will shoot on us. But the Israeli army would never shoot at rabbis. Would you be prepared to go there?' They said, 'But no one would accept the food from us.' I replied, 'The "terrorists" who are throwing stones at you, young Palestinians, will come and take the food from you.' They asked me if I was serious. I then telephoned Zogbi, a Christian in Bethlehem who is committed to non-violence. 'Zogbi, tomorrow morning at seven o'clock two lorries will arrive full of food. Find 20 strong young fellows to unload it and distribute it to Muslim and Christian families.' He asked me, 'But how will you get across the frontier?' I replied, 'You can stay on your side, and some rabbis will have got the lorries through.' 'That's impossible!' he said, 'It can't be true!' 'But it is,' I replied.

Next morning, at a quarter to seven, the rabbis telephoned me to say, 'We have arrived at the rendezvous, but no one's here.' I said, 'There is still a quarter of an hour. You must wait.' At exactly seven o'clock the young men came out from behind the wall and began to unload the lorries, not forgetting to offer a drink to the rabbis. In all, it took two hours. Later on, two of the rabbis came to see me. They had tears in their eyes – as indeed I had. They said to me, 'All our lives we have been trying to do some good, but the good you made us do today was worth everything we have tried to do all our lives until now. Now we know that it is possible to make peace.' There are many more examples I could give of things like that.

There is another story I would like to tell. In November I was on my way down from Beit Shean to Jericho. The Intifada was still extremely active and violent. Palestinians were being chased by Apache helicopters, which made for more casualties every day, and both sides were becoming more afraid of each other. On the one hand, the Jewish settlers were demanding a stronger military force to protect them; on the other the Palestinian extremists were not hesitating, whenever they could, to target 'a Jew', even a government minister, for assassination. I was taking an Australian in my car. It was raining slightly, the road was wet and the dust had turned into something like soap. It would not have been difficult to lose control of the vehicle. Suddenly, in the distance, we saw a car spin round and land up in the ditch on the side of the road. Fortunately, the ditch was not very deep. Then another car arrived and stopped. Five men got out of it and stood round the car that had broken down. They were five strong Palestinians. We stopped too when we got there. A young Jewish woman of about 30 was sitting in the car, apparently paralysed. The men asked her to get out, but the car windows remained closed and it seemed as if she was not reacting. The fright she had had from the accident was less than her fear of the five Palestinians. She did not know a word of Arabic, which was the only language they spoke. I went up to the car, smiled, and opened the door, all the time reassuring her and encouraging her to come out. 'They will not do you any harm, madam, all they want is to help you. Come out of the car and go and sit in mine while they get yours out of the ditch.' I stretched out my hand. After much hesitation, and doubtless still much afraid, she gave me her hand and came out to take refuge in my car. It took the men about ten minutes to get her car back on the road. Meanwhile, some soldiers arrived. The first thing they did was to point their guns at the Palestinians to interrogate them. At that moment the Jewish woman, forgetting her fear and her shock, opened the door of my car, rushed out and placed herself between the soldiers and the Palestinians shouting, 'What are you doing? Don't you see that they have just saved my life? Do you want to kill them? Put down your rifles!' The soldiers, caught off their guard by this reaction, told her to come and stand beside them. She refused, saying, 'Get away, I am not going to stand beside you but beside those who could

have killed me but instead protected me and comforted me.'
Fortunately, the soldiers understood. They let the Palestinians
go, and the woman for her part went off in her car. As for me,
I went on my way praying for peace between these blood
brothers.

The Jews are just like other people. They have a mind and
a heart. They can be moved to compassion. So can the
Palestinians. But when it is only weapons that are allowed to
speak, the noise of them gets in the way of any mutual understanding. And that leads to death. Unless we can walk together
we will be hung together. Walking together is not impossible.
Indeed we have lived together for 2,000 years, whether under
the Turks, or during the Crusades, or in the Nazi period. Arabs
and Jews can cohabit, they have always lived together. Today
we Palestinians are ready to live with the Jews. I profoundly
hope that Israel will flourish and I am ready to defend its
existence. On the other hand, I am incensed by the Palestinian
tragedy. I am incensed that thousands of men and women are
living in the Gaza desert and in refugee camps. We must find a
solution that is really just if we are to avoid repeating a still
greater injustice than that which was committed in 1948 when
the State of Israel was born.

For a certain period the Jews were regarded by Islam as
dhimmi, that is, as 'protected by the Prophet'. It was a status
accorded to Jews just as much as to Christian Arabs. In any case,
there has never been the kind of persecutions that have taken
place in France and in Europe. Jews have never been con-
sidered 'dirty Jews', only as people outside Islam. In certain
periods we Christians have been persecuted by Muslims much
more than the Jews have. But that does not mean that we
cannot live together.

We have to get back to the point of being open to what is possible. We have to recover our certainty that Jews and Palestinians can live together. Of course, one cannot expect a whole people to share this view, Nevertheless, it would not surprise me to find that the majority of the Palestinian people do share it. I am in contact with four or five thousand Palestinians every day. I know well the Palestinians in Gaza and the West Bank. I have been in touch with Palestinian refugees in Lebanon and in Jordan. And I know that the majority of Palestinians would enthusiastically welcome any solution which allowed them to recover a little dignity, an address and a home.

In the Israeli population the Jews are in the majority, but 1,300,000 citizens of Israel are Palestinian. So far as these Palestinians are concerned, you can be sure that, apart from a few small groups of Islamists or fanatics, the majority of them wish no harm to Israel and only want peace. We long for an independent Palestinian state, but we will continue to live in Galilee, in Haifa or in Nazareth. In the same way, the Jews in America want Israel to exist and be independent, but they do not all feel called to live there. Whatever anyone does, there will be Jews in a future Palestinian state and Palestinians in the present Jewish state. What is needed now is a normalization of the relations between the two peoples.

I regard Israel's destiny as linked to that of the Palestinians. Indeed the very independence of Israel seems to be intrinsically linked to that of the Palestinians. But this land of Palestine remains an ideal. It is not yet a reality. What it should be is a single entity in which Jews and Palestinians can live on equal terms, each having the same freedoms and each having the right to practise their religion. The Israeli Jews, just like the

Palestinians, think of their country's independence in the same terms as that of France or Germany. But Israel cannot be assured of its independence without the help of America and Europe. So how can Palestine? There is only one way to make this situation viable: to become interdependent partners, whether in the economy, in security, in education or in anything else. In this way the reunion of our two distinct but complementary countries in a single entity could be a model for the Near East and perhaps also for the rest of the world.

Today we need prophets like the great Isaiah to say to our Jewish brothers, 'You have the chance to be an embodiment of hope for the whole human race: do not miss it!'

4

The College of Mar Elias

In 1982 I wanted to do something for my village. We had no
secondary school. Half of the 8,000 inhabitants were under the
age of 14. Of these, only 90 could go to the secondary schools
in Haifa and Nazareth, and of these 90 only five or six were
girls. No one was interested in our village. So I went to see the
bishop of the time to ask him for help to start my project. What
he said to me was this: 'Do you want to put a pearl in a rubbish
tip like Ibillin? That is not something I can support. I certainly
shan't start a secondary school there.' So I had to follow a
different tack and do it on my own, without the bishop. Ibillin
was not, and never will be, a rubbish tip.

Nine months later, the first building was in place, four
storeys high. We had no building permit, but the building is
still there. We opened our doors on 1 September 1982 with 80
boys and girls aged 14 or 15 and four teachers, one of whom
was a woman. Eighteen years later, we expected 4,500 students
each 1 September.[1] Most of the students were Muslims; we also
had a number of Christians, a few Druze, and about 20 Jews. I

---

1 In September 2008 there were 1,250 children in the Kindergarten
and the Elementary School and 1,270 students in the High School. The
university college is now virtually empty since 'branch' universities are
being closed down and the Israeli government is witholding accreditation
from the college. [Editor]

told the Ministry of Education and the Israeli authorities that when their children came as our students they would not need any special provision: we were quite ready for them, and they would not be like strangers or guests, they would be members of the family. As for the teachers, we now had 285, of whom 85 had doctorates and 96 had Masters degrees. The others had four years of university study behind them. They were an elite body, all exceptional people. Most of them were Christians, but there were also a number of Muslims, a few Druze and 28 Jews. They were both men and women – which was nothing unusual, it is taken for granted. And now we have opened the first university for Arabs, Christians and Israelis – no, what am I saying? the first university for Israelis, Arabs and Christians – no, Christians, Israelis and Arabs . . . If I could find a word that would cover all three I would certainly use it. Together or separated, they all have the same place in my heart.

Today the secondary school has 1,600 pupils. There is also an upper school. Seven years ago we realized the importance of training a body of teachers capable of understanding the profound value of their gifts and of seeing teaching as a service to the community rather than as a source of prestige; and for four years we had a regional centre for the training of Arab teachers in Galilee, of whom there were 1,250.[2] We also decided to open the first Arab school for exceptionally gifted children. Most of that is still up and running. We are only at the beginning, but we are conscious that it is vital for the Jews and the Palestinians to have a mixed-race university where the differences and religious affiliations of all are respected. Today this

---

2 The Israeli government closed down all regional training centres in 2003. [Editor]

university exists at Ibillin, the smallest and least-regarded of the villages in Galilee. Our school now has more girls than boys, which is a significant statistic: with more girls than boys we have more chance of having families where the mother is educated and can pass on her education to her children. Ibillin is an oasis, a wonderful mosaic.

Many institutions have taken our school as a model. But at this moment there is no other one that can offer as many courses as we do, or which boasts such human and ethnic diversity.

Each year, before the children return, we have three days of training for the teaching staff. Each term, three days are given over to studying a topic that is discussed by the teachers. Every week there are meetings with those who are running classes. Those who need training receive it then; those who do not, can leave. If any refuse to be trained we have to dismiss them. It is true that the education we want to give to the children is based on acquiring knowledge, but this is not all. We also want to awaken the minds of our pupils and give them the desire to discover for themselves what they need to learn. This is why the teachers regularly receive training so that their teaching has this in view.

When I am standing in front of 800 or 900 teachers it is not them I see; it is the thousands of students behind them. My message of peace has to be taken by them into their homes. The philosophy of the school is based on respect of religious values and is intended to help men and women of different faiths to draw closer to each other. Our school does not belong to any denomination. It is not a place for drawing comparisons between one religion and another. The school also has a second objective: to raise awareness of the social and political state of affairs in Israel at the present time. We want our students to

develop a political awareness, and for this they need to understand the situation in as wide a perspective and in as objective a
manner as possible. In reality, time is a key factor: we are working for it and with it and against it. There is the time of the past,
which is memory; there is the time of the present, which is
what we are working on now; and there is the time of the
future, which is the vision of what is to come. The task for
today is to build that vision.

What we are doing here is crucial for the State of Israel. We
are bringing students and teachers from different political,
ethnic and religious backgrounds to live and work together.
This is how people begin to understand each other. It is all very
well to sign peace treaties, but the really difficult part is to write
them into the hearts of children around tables at school. That is
where peace is brought into being. A peace that is imposed at
the point of a bayonet is not real peace, it is simply a cease-fire.
It is not a matter now of tolerating each other, we have to
accept each other. What I am saying may not make political
sense; it may make no sense at all. But it is not our political
leaders who create a human community. Indeed it is often they
who destroy it. Here, at this school, our aim is to build it up.
Unity within diversity is the essential condition for survival in
the Holy Land.

But to come back to the school: it is a private school, it is
supported by no political party, not even by a church – my own
church or any other church. A film has been made about it: *A
Pearl on a Rubbish Heap* – the words the bishop used in 1982
when I told him that I wanted to build a school in Ibillin.

The struggle for permits

To begin with, getting to the point of building this school in Ibillin was a struggle. The first thing I did was go to the government to apply for a building permit. I had to wait for two weeks – and it was turned down. The reason given was that the site was not earmarked for the purpose – though it had belonged to us for 300 years! I was told, 'You have no money, you have no students, what is the use of building a school?' I was unconvinced by these arguments and decided it was better to do without a building permit. A few months later the police arrived and demanded to see my permit. I told them I had not got one. They asked me, 'But how are you building without a permit?' I replied, 'I have never used a permit for building, I have used sand, cement and water.' They lost their tempers and said, 'That is not how to behave in a civilized country!' I replied, 'If we were in a civilized country you would have given me a building permit. But apparently we are not – or not yet.' I was summoned to appear before a tribunal. I had to remember something that I have always tried to bear in mind – that these policemen have something in common with Arab, French, English, American and German policemen: behind the uniform there is a human being. I have always protested against police malpractice, but I have never felt hatred, only pity and a profound desire to get behind the uniform and lay bare the man, the young father, the uncle, the citizen.

To get the necessary political and financial support, I have often had to travel. I will tell you of just two of my journeys, the two most important ones.

By 1986 the school building had become much too small for

the number of children: the original 350 had been joined by another 750. The situation had become impossible. So I took the decision to create a new building – classrooms, workshops and a sports hall. The plans were prepared and the documentation was complete. The Minister of the Interior informed me: 'This time, Mr Chacour, you will get your permit. But you know our bureaucracy: it is likely to take time.' I let the ministry get on with the paperwork and began the building. A year later I received a visit from the police. They had been ordered by the tribunal to come and question me. Without a permit, I had to stop the work – which I did. But then, without delay, we began hollowing out the rock until we had three underground classrooms. I felt I could not send children back on to the streets to become illiterate and addicted to drugs and alcohol. Why should it make any difference that the state forbade me to build? That went on for six years. I knocked at the doors of ministers, junior ministers and various public figures. Every one of them was prepared to see me, but none of them gave me any help. By 1991 I was in utter despair and arrived at the conclusion that I would never get the building permit. So I took a big decision and bought an air ticket, the only one I have ever paid for myself. I left for Washington, and we landed at the National Airport, near the city centre. From there I took a car and went to see James Baker, who was at that time Secretary of State.

I knew that just then he had some disagreement with President Bush senior. Bush wanted to install extra security measures around all official residences, but James Baker thought they were unnecessary. Later on he told me, 'I wanted to live like other Americans and share the same risks. So I was against more security measures.' I thought this was remarkable and that he must be the kind of man who would understand me. I had no appointment, but I went and knocked at his door, thinking that they could hardly kill me and at worst would send me away. The door was opened by his wife Susan. He was not there. 'Who are you?' she asked. I replied, 'Madam, I am another man from Galilee.'

When she asked me whether I had an appointment, my answer was, 'Madam, we men of Galilee never have appointments, we just appear.' Later on she said to me, 'I don't know why I let you in; I was taken aback.' She invited me into the kitchen and offered me a glass of iced tea, a drink I have never much liked but which I thought it polite to accept. Sounds were coming from the sitting room. After only a few minutes she excused herself for not being able to spend longer with me. I would have to make an appointment to see her husband, the Secretary of State, and she promised to do her utmost to get me one. For the moment she was engaged with some American ladies studying the Bible. As she led me out, I asked her what part of the Bible they were studying. She replied that they were having a look at the Sermon on the Mount. I wished her good luck; and when she asked me why, I replied, 'Because you won't understand a word of it. In the first place, it was not written by an American but by someone from my country. Secondly, it wasn't written in your American language but in my Galilean dialect. So you will get it all wrong, and that is why I wished you good luck.' Susan Baker said to me, 'Could you help us to understand the text better?' What more could I have wished for? I spent the next two hours explaining to these handsome and generous American women what the Sermon on the Mount meant to me.

This is what I said: 'You must not imagine that Jesus Christ, my compatriot, would have dared to tell my ancestors the apostles to sit and do nothing when they were hungry and thirsty for justice. When the Jews drove my father out of his home, he had to walk to Nablus, cross the Jordan, go on to Amman in Jordan, to Damascus in Syria, to Beirut in Lebanon. When he met us again he told us that he had been so famished that he had had to eat earthworms and roots in order to survive. That is the spirit in which Jesus used to say to his disciples, "If you are hungry and thirsty for justice, get up, get moving and get your hands dirty for it." In the same way he never asked the fishermen on the Lake of Tiberias, who were my ancestors, to meditate on peace. Peace does not need people to meditate on it but to take action for it. It needs people with the courage to get up and get their hands dirty for it. So you must go and persuade your husbands to get their hands dirty – two fingers would be enough to bring peace to Israel.' I left the Bakers' house and stayed in Washington for 24 hours before returning home to Ibillin.

A week later the telephone rang. 'Father Chacour, could we say a prayer together?' And we did so. The same happened every week. We became prayer partners over the telephone – a typically American way of doing things. It quite often happened that when we were praying someone else would come on the line and say, 'Be quiet, the two of you. It's my turn to pray.' It was her husband, the Secretary of State. And the three of us prayed all together.

Three months later I remembered that when I went to Washington it was not to preach about the Sermon on the Mount or to pray by telephone but to get a building permit. So I telephoned Mrs Baker and asked her to write a letter to Shamir asking him to give me my long-awaited permit. She wrote a two-page letter and showed it to her husband. He said to her, 'No, you mustn't send that, it could cause a diplomatic crisis between Israel and the United States. Israel would pay no attention to your letter, and it's not a risk worth taking.' In his defence it must be said that this was happening just after the first Gulf War. Then he said to her, 'Give me the letter, I will add my signature, and I will take with me two copies of Abouna's books (I had become *Abouna* to them, which means their spiritual father). I will put them into Shamir's hands and ask him to give me the permit personally.' And that is how we got our permit to build the sports hall and some workshops, which are still in use today.

The real point is that one year later Mr and Mrs Baker decided to pay us a visit at the school. He had hardly got out of the car when he said, 'Abouna, I haven't come to visit you, I haven't just come to see you, I have come as an act of solidarity. I am doing it for our Palestinian Christian brothers. I am telling them to stay in their homes and in their villages because we need you here.'

Three months later we received a telephone call from the Israeli Ministry of Foreign Affairs to say that the Foreign Minister, Shimon Peres, who had received the Nobel peace prize, wanted to give a lecture in our Institute, to which of course I agreed. When I was introducing the Foreign Minister in the sports hall I told him the story of it. After a while he stopped me. 'Enough of that, please. I know this story down to the smallest details. I haven't come to talk about peace, I have come to find out why Mr Baker made merry hell in govern- ment circles in Jerusalem to get you a building permit. I simply wanted to see for myself, and now I have seen it. From now on you need not go to Mr Baker if you have a problem. I will be your ambassador myself.' Later on I wrote to ask him what sort of ambassador he hoped to be. He replied in his own hand, saying that usually he was an excellent ambassador. To tell the truth, he wasn't just excellent, he was extraordinary. I know that he persuaded, if not ordered, the Education Minister, Mr Rubinstein, to make a discreet visit to see what was happening at Ibillin. Six months before he came we had opened the university college, though it had not yet been officially recognized. When the Minister of Education came to Ibillin, he did not come empty handed. The gift he brought with him was worth all the gold in the world. It was his formal decision and official proclamation that we were now a recognized university college.

Victory!

Victory came – not just for me, but for him, for the Israeli people, for the Palestinians. This same minister – Mr Rubinstein – wrote me a letter a few weeks later saying, 'Now that you have official recognition, would you be prepared to accept as students some young Jews who have finished their military service?' What was I to say? I am a refugee, I have been deported, my village is in ruins and now I am asked to accept some Jewish soldiers. What I wrote in reply was this: 'You say you would like to send some ex-soldiers to study in my college. I beg you, send me the whole Israeli army! I would like to hold a discussion with them on two questions: how can they get rid of their weapons, and how are they to win over the hearts of Palestinian children with a smile of friendship and a spirit of sharing?' On the day that the first Israeli student arrived, I greeted him just like the others. Moments afterwards I was on my knees in my study, saying over and over again words that just came to me: 'Lord now lettest thou thy servant depart in peace. I know that they will come, because from now on they have no choice. All these young people want life, they have ambitions. They can only fulfil these ambitions if they will share them and live them out among us. And the sharing has already begun.'

I decided to make my second journey the day we began to build the lecture hall of the school. We had $200,000 and we needed another $300,000. On that very day I received a fax from Tokyo telling me that, to my great surprise, I had been awarded the Niwano peace prize – but on one condition: that I came to receive it myself in Tokyo. The prize was worth 20 million yen. Naturally I accepted, and with much gratitude, not least because this good news was brought to me by some Buddhists – and it was Buddhists (perhaps) who 2,000 years before had come to greet the birth of the Prince of Peace. This time it was their turn to be like princes of peace. So I left for New York with two companions, one a priest and the other a lady called Nawar who has been helping us for many years. We were received by an association of American doctors of Arab origin. They had arranged a splendid dinner for the occasion in honour of my college, the College of Elijah the Prophet. Among the 450 doctors there were Muslims, Christians and Druze. The proceeds of that evening amounted to $31,000, but the friendship they showed us was worth millions. Next day we took the plane to Indiana, where I was due to give a speech at the degree-giving ceremony of the University of Indianapolis and also to receive an honorary doctorate. I met the National Committee of Accreditation of American universities. The meeting lasted two hours, at the end of which we obtained recognition of our degrees by the Union of American Universities. It was an amazing experience.

Twenty-four hours later we took the plane for Tokyo. I can't imagine what had happened but when we arrived there after a 15-hour flight I was greeted like a prophet. The Minister of Education, the Chairman of the Niwano Prize and the leader of the Buddhists were at the airport to welcome me. They all made a deep bow to greet me and spoke their first words of greeting while they were still bowing. I was deeply moved by this. The next day they took me to see their Great Sacred Hall, the holy shrine of Buddhism. It is a grandiose building that will hold 10,000 people. I asked the officials who were with me what had brought all these people together. Was it a festival or was some famous person expected? The Minister of Education smiled and said, 'Yes, but that is nothing to do with you.' When the limousine stopped, no less than ten people came forward to open the door, and when I got out everyone began to applaud, and I realized that it was for me that all these people had come.

At the door of the temple there were ten Buddhist mothers. Each held a baby in her arms and each baby held a symbolic gift. I would have loved to kiss all these babies, but in Japan you do not kiss, you bow. It was a moving moment. Inside, the hall was packed. Two bonzes were kneeling in front of the Buddha and recited a prayer which lasted a quarter of an hour and in which several times I heard my name spoken. They prayed for me to be able to go on with my work in peace. But apart from my name I could not understand a word of what they were saying.

Next day came the peace prize giving ceremony. Two hundred and fifty distinguished Japanese were invited, among whom were several ambassadors. Four people gave speeches before me: first the Japanese Minister of Education, then the president of the Buddhist Niwano Association which had awarded me the prize, then the Israeli Ambassador to Japan, who (greatly to my surprise) was very complimentary about me, and lastly the Vatican Ambassador. Finally, it was my turn. They gave me a certificate and also a gift, which was a gold medal symbolizing Buddhism and a cheque for twenty million yen. I stayed in Japan for six days and then took the plane with my two companions back to the United States.

We landed at Atlanta, where I was expected at Emory University, one of the most prestigious in America. Its representatives wanted to award me a doctorate of theology. Around ten people were waiting for me at the airport, including the President and the Vice-President of the University. The very first thing they said to me was that my speech must not last more than five minutes. I replied that I had prepared one lasting 13 minutes. They retorted that there were 14,000 people receiving degrees and they could not authorize a speech longer than five minutes. I learnt the reason later: the Jewish community in Atlanta, knowing that I was Palestinian, had put pressure on the university. Luckily the President had refused to comply with their demand. He made one concession, which was to allow a Jewish woman to speak before I did. This Jewish woman, Deborah Liepstadt, was well known for her successful prosecution of David Irvine, the denier of the Holocaust, when he was on trial in England. After her speech vituperating against him, I began my own. It lasted four and a half minutes. I was applauded three times, and finally had a standing ovation for five minutes from the 14,000 people present. So I had my 13 minutes after all! This Jewish lady was deeply moved by what I said to her: 'I am a victim of yours and I appeal to the courage you have shown in not being moved from Germany to Palestine. We are paying the price of what others have done to you. I don't want to be the Jews' "Jew". I am your long-lost brother, and what I am saying comes from a heart that knows only love.' In the end she came and kissed me. It was truly a beautiful and moving moment.

While we were putting up the last building in the school I received a large number of letters of support. Sometimes they even contained a cheque. Once I had a letter from a lady of 80, which said, 'I have read your books, I totally support what you are doing, and so I have decided to send you all that I have been able to save during the last month.' She enclosed a cheque for $10. One of the classrooms will be named after her: she had given us all that she had saved.

A few months after the completion of the sports hall I had a telephone call from a lady who said, 'I have been wanting to come and see you for four years, but I have never dared to. Everyone dissuaded me, saying you were always abroad, and that you were terribly busy and would not have time to see me. But I would love to come with my daughter. Would that be possible?' I said, 'Of course, come tomorrow morning.' When she came I showed her the sports hall and told her its history. Leaving it from the other side I told her about a project for a building of three or four storeys with a bridge joining the sports hall to the terrace in front of it. She said that she thought it was an excellent idea, and out of curiosity asked me how much I thought it would cost. I replied that I was not thinking of that: it would be something for my successor to do. But when she insisted that she wanted to know ('just out of interest'), I said that one would have to allow $65,000–75,000 for a building on this scale. We went to have a cup of coffee with her daughter. At one point she said to her, 'My dear, get out your cheque book and write Mr Chacour a cheque for $65,000.' When she came back a year later we asked her to unveil a stone plaque with an inscription. It bore the name of her family: MASON BRIDGE.

The new generation

I have been doing some research on the Arab community in Israel, and I have discovered some marvellous things, but also some dangerous ones. In our communities 75 per cent are less than 28 years old, 50 per cent are less than 14. I can see an extraordinary potential in these figures. Our hope lies in all these young people whom we, the adults, must prepare for the dialogue which they will be having with their Jewish brothers and sisters. Once they are grown up all these young people will have the chance to establish a genuine peace. On the other hand, if we allow this young generation to grow up in bitterness and deprivation, the ineluctable result will be violence and war.

Education plays a crucial role in the formation of attitudes. The segregation of schools in Israel, where Arabic is taught as the language of the enemy, is very dangerous. The reproach that can be made to Palestinians applies equally to the Israelis. It is better to make a change in oneself than always to be accusing others. This makes me think of a Palestinian mother who one day takes her son to the beach. When he is there he meets a little Jewish child and begins playing with him. His mother says to him, 'Youssef, come here! Why are you playing with that

Jew?' 'But Mama, he isn't a Jew, he is a child!' Before we were ever Jews, Muslims or Palestinians we were simply men and women. We must always remember our common identity. The trouble is that we educate our children, not to be human beings, but to be Zionists, or left wing, or right wing, or Palestinian fanatics standing on their rights with hatred in their hearts. Let us stop throwing stones at each other and resorting to guns; let us, the adults, join hands so as to give a different kind of education to our children, an education that will allow them to come to terms with each other, to get to know each other and to appreciate each other. David is a boy in my school. He is no longer 'a' Jew, he is 'my' Jew, my friend.

5

A Holy Land – A Chosen People?

The land

Abraham is buried in the town of Hebron. Abraham the patriarch belongs to us all. The Muslims have great respect for him: they call him the Friend of God. My hope is that one day Israel will feel able to adopt the Muslim name of this town: Al-khalil, which means 'Friend'. Hebron is the Town of the Friend *par excellence*. If Israel would give Hebron its Muslim name it would already be a token of reconciliation. Abraham is the father of all of us. We hold him in common, and we Palestinians are ready to be reconciled to honour his memory. We are ready to do it – though not, of course, at any price.

I believe that Zionism has convinced the majority of Jews that this land belongs to them. They know that the Palestinians live there, but many of them say to us that we were there just to look after it until they returned. Now that they have returned and taken possession of it they are asking us to leave. That this is a 'land without a people which belongs to a people without a land' (the 'land' being Palestine, the 'people' being the Jewish nation) is a misconception they cannot get rid of. Unfortunately for the Jews, and fortunately for us Palestinians, we are not latecomers: we did not arrive after the creation of the State of Israel, we were there before, and it is the creation of the State of Israel that has forced us to leave. The Palestinians cannot forget that Palestine is their land too. They have made a real concession in accepting that Israel should occupy 78 per cent of their land, but they insist the rest should be given back. It would hardly be an act of charity if Israel were to give us back 20–24 per cent of our land. It would be no more than the minimum, but it would make possible a solution that had some element of justice. Our Jewish friends seem unable to understand this. They have tried to convince the whole world that the Palestinians are simply troublemakers, envious thieves who ought to go and live with other Arabs. By dint of this they have ended up believing and being convinced of the greatest untruth of the twentieth century: that the Palestinians do not exist!

The Jewish people claim that they have the right to return to the land of Palestine after 2,000 years. My response to this is another question: Why not go back 4,000 years, when Abraham left Iraq? The Jews claim Abraham as their forefather, which is true. But why then do they not understand that Abraham was not a Jew but an Arab? According to the Talmud, he says it himself: 'I am a heathen living among a heathen people.' The belief that this land was given to them by God is peculiar to the Jews. The Muslims, for their part, have as part of their faith the doctrine that every land that has ever been Muslim must remain so for ever. For me, who am not a Jew but a Christian, the land is not important. It is not something sacred. I do not believe in a 'Holy Land'. It is only the people who should become holy. The problem with the Jews is that they believe that Palestine is their promised land and will not allow other peoples to make the same claim in the name of their own religion. In the case of Palestine, Abraham belongs as much to the Muslims as to the Jews. Both worship the same God, the God of Abraham, Isaac and Jacob.

My Christian vision and my Christian theology give me a different answer. Who is invited to the heavenly banquet? In my belief, it is not Jews or Muslims or Christians, it is every man and every woman created in the image of God. We should ask the Jews whether they think of themselves as, first and foremost, human beings. If they answer yes, then they are honoured guests, elect and chosen just as we are. But if they reply no, then we have a very serious problem. Recently, we have had a Pope in Rome who had the courage to tell us that it is to our neighbours, who may be neither Christians nor Catholics, that we should look for help in strengthening our faith and finding a deeper meaning in life. Human complementarity is something which must evolve irreversibly if we are to survive. We live in a society that has no belief in a particular divinity or a particular God. Hence it is impossible to lay claim to a land as divinely given. When one finds other religions making the same claims and the same affirmations, one has to ask who is right and who is wrong. Is the Muslim being realistic when he interprets the Qu'ran as saying that Muslim land must always remain Muslim? Are the Jews correct in claiming that this land is an exclusive gift from God? I think both are wrong. No land is either Jewish or Muslim. No land belongs to Islam or to Judaism. What both Islam and Judaism have to learn is to belong to a single land and to share it in partnership.

The people

When Israel tries to use military force to impose its own religion, it is doing something that is incompatible with today's society. It is no longer the case that only the Jews were the true authors of history. They are no longer the only people who know how to read and write. Israel must come up to date and become a member of the human race on an equal footing with everyone else. After the assassination of Rabin by a fanatical Jew, I read this striking comment: 'State of Israel, Jews the world over – welcome into the human community!' This was as much as to say: 'You have been trying to convince us that a Jew never kills a Jew. But now you are killing each other.' I should have preferred to say, 'Welcome, our well-beloved brothers and sisters, you who have suffered so much; welcome, our well-beloved brothers and sisters who have made others suffer so much; brothers and sisters who need both to be healed yourselves and to bring healing to others – welcome, well-beloved, into the human community. Otherwise there is no hope.'

I fear I have to say that the monotheistic religions have let us down. Islam, Judaism and Christianity have failed to be instruments of peace. I believe one has to distinguish between religious practice and the values held in common by the three religions. It is not enough to believe in the one God. One has to be able to recognize God in one's conscience. A Jewish rabbi, a Muslim sheik and a Christian priest can do something together, but in their own name, not in the name of their religion. However much we respect the need for pluralism and diversity, we have to leave religion out of it. At present we just tolerate one another, because we have not yet reached the point of accepting one another. At an early stage, Hitler just tolerated the Jews. But he never accepted them, he never thought of them positively. Like Herod, he bided his time until he had found 'the final solution'. We have to move beyond tolerance to the point of accepting one another, which means accepting that the other is different and that this difference is an enrichment, not a threat. That is the way our attitudes have to evolve, and unfortunately it is not yet happening.

I repeat: the monotheistic religions have not been instruments of peace. Indeed in the course of history they have rather been sources of division. I asked one of my former teachers at the Hebrew University, who was Dean of the Faculty of Humanities, to give a lecture to my Arab students on the meaning of the Jews as the Chosen People. This distinguished Professor Werblowski then asked me, 'Do you want me to teach them about the origins of apartheid?' This gave me much food for thought. Being 'chosen' may have some advantages, but it is also somewhat uncomfortable, especially if you come to think that it is a privilege that makes you superior to others who are *not* chosen. It is a state of mind which can make you say, 'You may be very good people, but I am a bit better: you are all human beings, but I have privileged access to the divine.' But we are all human beings. The very fact of thinking oneself superior exposes one to rejection and persecution. As a Christian today in Israel, in the Holy Land, I live among a majority of Muslims and a still larger majority of Jews. Questions of survival, of the future, of co-operation come back to haunt me every day. How can we achieve equality and partnership? From within the point of view of just one religion, it is hard to conceive a way forward.

The Jewish religion makes a distinction between Jew and *goy*, between elect and pagan. According to this conception, therefore, one is born either one or the other. One's birth as one of the elect confers a sense of superiority and consequently becomes a source of segregation. This brings with it a host of problems. If we follow the teachings of the Talmud and the Old Testament, we have to believe that non-Jews have a future with Jews, but only so long as they are willing to think of themselves as inferior. They will never fully belong to the family of the nation, the society and the religion. They will always be visitors and guests. Only those who belong in the household are members of the family. In Israel, unfortunately, this conception has been applied to exclude us Christians, us Palestinians. After the terrible holocaust inflicted on our Jewish brothers, those who arrived in Israel had this attitude towards us. The great majority of us were deported – an almost complete ethnic cleansing. 'Almost complete', because there was left here the 'little bit of filth', which is how we Israeli Arabs are thought of. And what they say to us today is, 'We will tolerate you here, on condition that you accept being visitors and foreigners.' But this is impossible. We cannot think of ourselves as foreigners in our own home. It is rather we who have welcomed the 'new arrivals', *oliem hadashiem*, into our land of Palestine. We are not intruders, and we cannot accept being given the status of intruders who should be got rid of. We are like Naboth in the Bible. Naboth had the right to his vineyard near the King of Israel. Killing Naboth, or forcing him to leave his vineyard and appropriating it against his will, amounted to incurring the divine wrath and risking a death still more horrible than that which was visited on poor Naboth, whose advocate and protector was this same God of Israel.

The most complex and serious question is this: Can we imagine a Judaism that fully accepts that the Palestinians are not foreigners in Israel but are an integral part of the state, of the nation – that they belong to this land as much as the Jews do, if not more? Can we imagine an Islam that does not divide the world into believers and non-believers? True, according to the Prophet, non-believers should be protected; but in reality they are not so much protected as tolerated, since it is they who pay the taxes that support the army, and the army's task is to spread Islam. Today these are deep-rooted attitudes – you are non-believers, you are infidels, you do not belong to the family! These are serious matters, for in these circumstances how can one talk of 'democracy' or 'sharing responsibility'?

The Christian record

Our record as Christians is not much more creditable. When, in the time of our immaturity, we claimed that there is no salvation apart from baptism, what did we do to make our message comprehensible? We splashed people with water and told them that was it, that was baptism! What did the missionaries do who came to the Holy Land as recently as the 1930s to convert the poor Muslims to Christianity? They gave a two shilling piece to the little Muslims on condition that they said after them, 'Blessed be Jesus'. So they repeated, 'Blessed be Jesus'. When the children went home they said to their mothers, 'Look, I have got some money. We can buy some food.' Their mothers asked them where this money came from, and they told them how they had got it. Then the mothers said, 'This money is worthless. Throw it away and say, "Cursed be

Jesus!'" Is that the way to do mission? What about the way of Basil the Great, who when he was Patriarch of Constantinople at the end of the fourth century got rid of all the wealth of his church in order to build villages and a hospital, the famous 'Basiliad', for slaves who had been expelled from Rome? Basil the Great did not baptize them. If people asked for baptism, the first thing was to teach them Christian principles. Unfortunately, we have failed to understand this. For us, baptism amounts to putting a little water on a person's head and making a pretence of prayer in much the same way as pagans pray to their gods. That, we think, guarantees salvation. What does conversion mean? Or confession? Or forgiveness? Forgiveness is not so easy. It implies a real conversion, a change of direction. Without that, forgiveness has no value. Everything depends on what one does and not on what one thinks. It is not easy to be a good Christian, but it is quite easy to exploit Christianity for one's own ends, which have nothing to do with God and with what he expects of us.

There was a time when we Christians almost ceased to be human, claiming that without baptism no one could be saved. We thought of baptism as a privilege rather than as an act of God's grace. But which baptism? Reformed, re-reformed, or unreformed? The question resulted in the wars of religion. In any case, if it is only Christians who go to heaven, I think God prefers to go to hell with the rest of humanity! For God created human beings out of love, compassion and mercy; he made us for life and survival, not for damnation in hell. Who are we to say that those who have not been baptized will go to hell? Who gave us authority to judge others? Who said to us, 'You are judges of this world'? What allows us to say that our followers will be saved and the rest will be damned? I cannot find anything like it in the teaching of Jesus Christ. Jesus did not condemn the prostitute or the centurion of Capernaum or the rich man. Jesus did not condemn anyone, for he came to save us, not to condemn sinners. We have gone astray by putting people into a category according to whether they have or have not done something that in itself cannot save any of us, as if baptism were automatically sufficient for salvation. To be saved we have to meet our obligations, not just once, but every day. If heaven and hell exist, I am quite sure there will be many baptized Christians who will go to hell. To have any hope of salvation we have to follow Jesus Christ and walk in his footsteps as his disciples did.

To come back to this idea of election: there is something I want to add. The fact of thinking oneself to be one of the elect, and therefore different from others and better than others, often brings about jealousy and hatred. I think that is one of the reasons why the Jews have been so often persecuted in the course of history.

God has endowed human beings with a nature that drives them to pursue the freedom and equality that is needed for flourishing. Everything that puts us back into slavery, subordination, marginalization or poverty is opposed to human nature. We were created to experience joy and to achieve a certain fulfilment, not to make each other suffer hardship. The teaching of Jesus Christ, my Master, is about love and happiness. I want to appeal to all my Jewish, Christian and Muslim brothers and sisters to take to heart these words of the Lord: 'Any of you who want to be first should sit in the lowest place. Any of you who want to be leader should become the servant of all.' We must not talk about being damned or being saved. It is only after our lives are over that we shall know whether we have deserved to be saved or not. Therefore we must make every effort to follow the Lord despite the temptation to follow our own bidding. It follows that the Jewish idea of elect Jews on one side and *goyim* on the other, the Muslim idea of believers on one side and infidels on the other — neither has any place in the context of Jesus' teaching.

This is not a matter of looking out for a chance to proselytize. I tell Jews to remain as Jews and Muslims to remain as Muslims. Jesus Christ has taught me that you are worthy to be loved as you are, you have the right to be different from me and you will still be loved. It is only by accepting you, loving you and witnessing to my own faith in Christ before you that I can be saved. My ambition — a wild one — is to convert all Jews and all Muslims, not to Christianity, but to God. God alone knows their destiny. I want the Jews to become really good Jews, not fundamentalists or fanatics; and I want the same for Muslims.

Election

The concept of election is very dangerous. I hesitate to say it, but my conscience will not allow me not to. Hitler made use of this concept of election: the elect were the Aryans. His slogan was, 'God is with us'. To hell with the Jews, to hell with the gypsies, to hell with the Africans, to hell with the Arabs . . . to hell with everyone save the Aryans. When the Turks massacred one and a half million Armenians in the space of two years (1915–17) it was because they thought Turkish blood was superior to that of the Armenians.

For the Jews, the Talmud is essentially a commentary on certain biblical principles. You could compare it with the Christian casuistry of the Middle Ages. Sometimes I am shocked by its teaching. One of the shocking things is what it says about Christianity; for example, the comparison between a Christian and a pig: 'Which is better? a Christian or a pig?', to which the answer is, 'The pig, because pigs do not convert Jews.' But this kind of attitude, which we find in the Talmud, is simply the result of persecutions. There is a powerful impulse in it to be distinguished from others, not to be like other nations. What is serious about it is that it engenders a certain suspicion towards non-Jews, who must be respected but also suspected, and so cannot be friends, cannot be absolutely trusted.

This state of mind goes beyond relations between Jews and *goyim*. It affects the way you think of your wife, your daughter, your brother, your neighbour, your colleague. You end up suspecting instead of respecting. What a contrast with what that other man said: 'My friends, you are my disciples. If someone makes you go one mile, go with him two; if someone wants your tunic, give your cloak as well. Give without expecting any return.' This is the very basis of Jesus' teaching. He invites us to be, not suspicious, but respectful. Your brother may insult you once, twice, 40 times, and you must still forgive him. I try to apply this in my daily life. When a Jew calls on me I am not suspicious of his intentions. I do all I can to respect him as a person and I listen to him so as to be able to discover what is best in him. I begin by telling him that he is not a visitor but a member of the family. It must be wretched to live with people whom one is always being suspicious of. That way one can never be at peace in oneself.

A year ago I had to give a lecture. It was in what is called a 'discussion panel'. Among those present was the chief rabbi of the town of Safed and a Muslim sheik. As I had come in last and was the least important of the three I was asked to speak last. The rabbi gave an excellent talk on the positive side of Judaism, on how it is self-sufficient so long as one adheres to it strictly. The sheik then quoted the words of Muhammad, to the effect that in order to be saved one must become a Muslim. When it was my turn, I said, 'Listen, Mr Rabbi: There are certainly many differences between us, and these are matters of doctrine. It is difficult for us to accept each other as things are. Nevertheless, we Christians belong to a branch that stemmed from Judaism and there is much we have in common: your prophets are my prophets, your psalms are my psalms, most of your prayers are my prayers. The only real matter of disagreement between us is the coming of the Messiah, Jesus Christ. You say that the Messiah is to come, I say that he has already come. My proposal to you is that we should work together in harmony to create a human society in which it will be good to be alive. Then he will be able to tell us whether he is coming (as you believe) or whether he has come and is coming back (as we believe). Neither you nor I nor our friend the sheik was born a Christian, a Muslim or a Jew. According to the Bible, we were born first and foremost as children, created in the image of God.' The rabbi got up and left the room.

It is much the same with fundamentalism in Islam, which uses language that is excessively brutal and exclusive. Afghanistan is a striking example. So is Iran. The menfolk are half blind, the way they prevent the women from emancipating themselves. It is a society where it is difficult to live. The traditionalist conception of Islam has little in common with the teaching of the Prophet. As for Judaism, one wonders whether it can succeed in creating a secular state that will respect religious principles but not religious fanaticism. At least we Christians have moved some distance away from the idea that we are superior. The best Christian community is one that defines itself as a community of sinners asking God's forgiveness. A community of sinners cannot possibly be superior, it can only be a community called to be at the service of others.

6

A Personal Faith

All these contradictions I find to be the mirror image of my own identity. In reality I am a Palestinian, an Arab and a Christian, all three – none of which began in the West, however much some people have tried to persuade me otherwise. Christianity is not a western phenomenon. Moreover, I am also an Israeli citizen. These things are incompatible, and yet these four definitions are true of me all the time. Of these facets that make up my identity I cannot decide to give preference to one over the others. The day that I discovered I was not born a Christian was the happiest day of my life. It was the day I realized that we are not born Jews or Christians or Muslims but simply babies in the likeness of God. This has helped me to solve many problems. I thank God and all the heavenly powers for allowing me to discover this. It enables me to bear the weight of all the contradictions that are in me. I do not pretend that I am at peace with myself, I am always tempted to give preference to one facet or another, to choose the easiest solution. It is a perpetual struggle that I have to wage within myself, and sometimes it prostrates me.

In 1970 I had had enough. I had plenty of enthusiasm, I had been a priest just four years. But it seemed to me that everything was out of kilter – church, state, society, even my own parish. It was only myself, I thought, that was all right. So I decided to get away from it all in order to preserve anything good that still remained in me. I left to go to Geneva, in Switzerland, where I taught at Bossey, the ecumenical institute of the World Council of Churches. At that time its Principal was Professor Nissyotis, who has since died. My idea was that I would be out of reach and would be able to maintain my integrity away from those wretched Jews, those wretched Palestinians, those wretched Arabs and those wretched churches. I stayed there just a month. One evening, I gave a lecture in front of about 40 specialists in ecumenism. While I was speaking to them about pluralism in society, I realized that any European could give a lecture like the one I was giving and would certainly do it much better; but at Ibillin, who could do it? Certainly, none of these 40 specialists. This thought worried me deeply. I reviewed my position, and the result was I took the decision to return to Palestine, where I have been ever since. I love the Jews, the Muslims, the Christians with all their problems. Indeed, often I love them *because of* their problems. Our conflict is not something outside ourselves: little by little we *become* the conflict. The good and the evil are in us. The choice is ours, and the future depends on what we choose.

Without my faith, I do not know how I could have survived. I need Jesus Christ. I need very often to withdraw and talk with him. In the face of one situation or another I often ask myself: how would he have acted? When I arrived at Ibillin 36 years ago, it was a primitive village where everything had to be done from scratch. Every Sunday I used to say to my parishioners, 'I know you often pass the church, which is right in the centre of the village. In the presbytery, which is now my house, you will always see a light. I leave it lit on purpose so that whenever you want to, you can knock at the door and come in.' When three

St Joseph nuns came here, Mother Makeer, who has died now, said to me, 'But, Abouna, you have to rest. People are coming to disturb you all the time, even when you are having a meal or sleeping. It is too tiring for you. Fix certain times for letting them come and keep certain times for yourself.' I replied without thinking, 'But tell me, sister, suppose you were very tired and having a rest and someone knocked at your door and you asked who it was and someone replied, "I am Jesus Christ, I need to see you." Would you ask him to wait until you had finished your rest? He is on the road that leads to the cross, he will not come back and you will never see him again. Won't you get up to let him in?' She replied, 'But for Jesus, that's different.' I said there was no way it was different. Jesus Christ is not different from our village people, our parishioners, our Jews and Muslims. Every time one of them comes here, it is Jesus that I am asking in. Apart from that, nothing matters, not eating or sleeping. It is my privilege to ask them in. Of course it is difficult at times, and sometimes it is very hard indeed. But never forget that Jesus had nowhere to lay his head.

If God had not given me my faith I would have abandoned the priesthood long ago. I would have disowned all that the Church stands for. It is not enough to say, 'I have faith', one has to be *in* faith. Faith is not something one loses and then finds again. Faith means continuity in Jesus Christ. We either follow him or we don't. If we turn away from him, it is like getting lost. But he is always waiting for us. He is waiting for us with tears, with longing and with impatience, like the good father waiting for the return of the prodigal son. That father was hoping for just one thing: the return of his son alive. He never worried about the money that his son had squandered, about the bad name he had made for himself, about the shame he had brought on the family. When the boy returned home, he did not even give him time to speak. He said to him, 'Say nothing now, just follow me. You were dead and now you are alive. You were lost and now you are found. You will not be a slave now. You will have your dignity again.' He went on, 'Let him be bathed, and let him be dressed in the finest clothes and given the finest ring. My son has come home: he is my pride, my well-beloved son.' That is what faith means. When God gives you faith, he makes you a free gift of his grace. He lets you walk in a darkness that has light in it. You cannot see that light, but you can follow the one who walks through the darkness and will lead you to the light. We have to learn to lose ourselves in that light. We cannot bargain with God. It is not a matter of praying for five minutes a day, or an hour and a half, or two and a half. It is a matter of praying day and night, at every moment of one's life. One must do everything as if one was constantly in the Lord's presence. When I have a meal with the West Bank workmen who are building the hall and the church – their presence there is illegal because the State of Israel has not given us a building permit – I am praying just by being with them, eating with them. Their smile is part of my prayer. But there is more. When they and I have got back home I have to concentrate on conversing with the one whom I believe to be alive, the one who is never absent. The one who *is* absent is very often myself. Not that he is ever angry with me: he is simply waiting for me to give place to him so that he can go in front of me to show me the way. For he *is* the way, he *is* the light.

The nature of faith

Faith is not belief. Faith is not just believing that Jesus Christ is our saviour, that God is a Trinity, that Mary is the Mother of God. If our faith stops there – pity us! We shall be condemned to a miserable existence. Faith is the Incarnation. In other words, we have to identify ourselves with those who share our life, with those whom we believe in – with Jesus Christ.

This is why Christians in the West tend to despise us Palestinian Christians: we are not sufficiently interested in philosophy and theology. We are too busy telling a story. Stories are what you tell small children, not great scholars. And yet I have noticed the greatest scholars thirsting to hear a story. They have had enough of thinking about abstractions, principles, philosophical trends – all of which may be very interesting, but they are not real life. As for us, we have a story to tell, a true story. We have in our possession two things that do not exist anywhere else: an empty tomb and a man risen from the dead! It is an extraordinary story, but it is the story of our life, it is the story of life itself. I could take you into Galilee for a walk with the Lord, with Jesus, my compatriot, a man of Galilee. For those who believe in Jesus, for those who really have faith, there is no question of privileges, preferences, differences, because we are all called to become the adopted children of God. That means that we have to change our behaviour. It puts an end to nationality, to belonging to such and such a religious community, to being a chosen people – we are all invited to the same banquet, but not for any of these reasons, only because we are a man or a woman.

So we have to understand that Christianity is not a matter of philosophy, a theological pursuit. We have to learn a lesson from the Christians of Byzantium. They were philosophers and theologians of the highest discernment. They were committed and sincere. When the Arabs laid siege to Constantinople, they did not stir because they were much too busy debating how many angels can dance on the head of a pin. But in the mean time Constantinople had fallen for ever.

Jesus has to be my friend before he is my Lord. He said it himself: 'I do not call you slaves; I call you my friends.' Jesus is always speaking to me. I can go without food, but I cannot go without conversing with him who has turned my life upside down, who has disturbed my human tranquillity and helped me to find a peace which embraces suffering. That is what prayer is, that is what faith is.

For me, the only matters of real importance are God and human beings. Human beings have evolved within the beauty of the cosmos. The word 'cosmos' has given rise to the idea of 'cosmetics'. It is unfortunate that so many women want to make themselves even more beautiful than God has created them to be. It is something they cannot ever achieve. However much they paint themselves, they will never become more beautiful. Our bodies are beautiful as they are. Come and sit in my garden around five o'clock in the evening. You will hear thousands of birds singing at the close of the day. Byzantine iconography interprets the whole cosmos: the Holy Spirit is spread abroad not only in our hearts but throughout creation. God is not Christian – that statement infuriates many Christians. But my question is: What sort of Christian do you think he ought to be? Roman Catholic? Melkite Catholic? Protestant? Reformed? God is our Creator, and the calling of Christians is to reflect his presence among ourselves so that others can see him. By that I do not mean that God is Muslim or Jewish. That would be equally fatuous. Jews and Muslims are no better than we are so far as parties and sects and every kind of division are concerned. God does not kill. God gives life and abolishes death, giving us the chance to transform our lives into eternal life. We have the choice, either to stay close to God or to stray far from him, to be a reflection of his love or of our own egoism – in which case we are saying to God, 'Go back where you were, I wish to be independent.' If we believe that God is the source of life but still go on like that, we are choosing death. I believe that drawing close to God and allowing oneself to be filled with the divine presence is to become truly rooted in life. That is why we say that those who have departed before us are not dead and buried but rest in peace with the Lord, in the hope of the resurrection. God was willing to be crucified to give us life. Christianity is not morbid, it does not glorify martyrdom, though if the choice is between losing one's life and rejecting God, then martyrdom may be the path to choose. We must always do everything we can to escape persecution. But if we are driven to it we may well have to choose between deserting God in order to live or holding on to our faith in order to begin a new life in his presence.

We must not put the cart before the horse. Peace is not an end in itself. Peace is the result of something else. What we are talking about is something that spreads and irradiates. In order to educate people for peace one must first sharpen their sense of justice and integrity. They must learn to respect themselves through the respect they will show to others. I am very fond of the Hebrew word *shalom*, which is the same in Aramaic (*shlomo*) and in Arabic (*salaam*). These three words mean the same thing: complete, perfect, whole. *Shalem*, the root of the Hebrew word *shalom*, has two meanings: 'to pay', and 'perfect'.

This means that if you want peace you have to pay for it. And the price of peace is pluralism, diversity, accepting that others are different. The word *shalom* can also take the form *shlemut*, which means 'a clear conscience'. It makes no difference if you are being persecuted, you can still have *salaam*, *shalom*, *shlomo* and a conscience at peace. The odd thing is that when you are looking for peace you often have to pay for it with your own blood. Mahatma Gandhi sealed his search for peace with his blood; he was murdered by an Indian. Martin Luther King did the same: he sealed his non-violent struggle with his blood; he was killed by a black man. Oscar Romero too was killed by one of his compatriots. All these men paid for their search for peace with their blood, with their life. Were they not inspired by the Sermon on the Mount?

7

The Tragic Guilt of the West

It is unfortunate that, because of what happened in the course of the Second World War, the West has its hands tied. I believe that if Europe could free itself from this sense of guilt, which originates in the consequences of that war, and could sharpen its sense of responsibility for the conflict which exists today in Israel, it could play a decisive role where the United States is disqualified from doing so. The United States has acknowledged its culpability, and its unilateral position follows from that. It has taken sides. The Americans have the skills, but they do not have the culture. They have the power, but not the moral sense: a senator will do anything to be elected and re-elected and to get the money needed for the electoral campaign. Hillary Clinton said that the settlements were illegal, but once she became a senator this was completely forgotten. There are plenty of senators who have sold their principles to keep their seats. Of those who have dared to speak up and publish the truth, I know of seven who have lost their seats and have never been re-elected. Yes, Europe has a role to play, but it has to become mature enough to play it. It must make a clear distinction between anti-Zionism and anti-Semitism. To criticize Israel is not to be anti-Semitic, any more than supporting Israel means being anti-Palestinian. For the moment, Europe seems paralysed by its official policy. But there is a gulf between the people and their governments. The freedom of speech allowed to governments seems a great deal less than that allowed to their peoples. That is alarming, because I remember those dark times when criticism of the Jews became widespread and then turned into bitterness and denial, bringing in its train the persecutions we know so well, the Holocaust. I tell the Jews to be careful about their military power, which, far from working for them, in fact makes it more difficult for them to be integrated into the international community.

The developing countries have a sense of being ill-treated by the West. Some research was done some ten years ago on the aid being given by the United States. The conclusion was that American financial aid to the developing countries amounted to $5 billion and the profits gained from them amounted to 15 billion! This raises the question, Who is helping whom? We are not much in love with the foreign policy of the United States, which shows no respect for poor countries: its exports consist mainly of armaments and money.

During Reagan's presidency I asked the former president Jimmy Carter to intercede with him to stop the transfer of arms to us. If he was determined to send us something, several thousand copies of the American Constitution would have been more acceptable. He replied candidly that this was one thing that the White House did not like to export! It is true that it is easier to manipulate a totalitarian power, which does what it likes and is accountable to no one, than to negotiate with a people in a democratic system, who may oppose anything that diminishes their rights.

Despite the horrible experience that America endured in 2001, it must make an effort to understand why poorer countries find its foreign policy unacceptable. Why does it have so many enemies at the same time as it believes it is being generous? Why do the recipients of its generosity continue to bear a grudge against it? America has to examine its conscience – Europe also. Developing countries need not only bread, they need dignity and respect. Western armaments give them neither one nor the other.

I recall a lecture I gave at Ibillin some 15 years ago. The audience consisted of communists and some senior Israeli officials. One of these officials began very arrogantly to lecture the communists, accusing them of anti-government activity and of fomenting strikes. In short, he told them to shut up. One of the communists, an old man, rose to his feet, saying, 'Education Inspector, what you say may be true, but the tone of your words lacks humility, we are not impressed by it! A little more humility . . .' The attitude of the United States towards the developing countries is rather like that of this inspector. And this is the problem. No American has chosen to be American, any more than any Palestinian has chosen to be Palestinian. One does not choose one's family. On the contrary, we have to remember that we all belong to the same great family, that of the human race. We are all children with the same life, a life we have to share with one another.

When Madeleine Albright, who was then Secretary of State, came to Jerusalem, I asked her, 'Tell me, Mrs Albright, why don't you treat Israel as you have treated Iraq and other countries when they violated human rights?' She replied, 'You don't punish your friends.' I hardly think that is a valid argument. If I have a friend who is a crook, ought I to protect him? If I have a friend who is a robber, ought I to give him my blessing? By no means. If he is a good man I encourage him. If he is bad, I reproach him. That is a lesson for today. It may be too much like peasant wisdom for people who have too much money, who live in skyscrapers so that their feet never touch the ground. These people will never be able to understand what compassion is. For compassion means, first, respecting oneself, and then, above all, respecting others.

We need to use a language that is a bit more human. We are not living in the jungle. For the purpose of killing each other we have bombs, aircraft, helicopters – and everyone is living in a nightmare, not least the United States and Europe. Today, anyone who has access to chemical weapons can wipe Europe off the map. In the United States the tiniest aircraft used to spray insecticides is forbidden to fly, in case instead of insecticide it has 'humanicide'. Where have we ended up? Let us ask ourselves some questions. Who makes these terrible weapons? Who exports weapons of such destructive power? What sort of places are Europe and America who export the poison along with the cure? The Middle East has not even the resources to make a needle, they have to be brought from France or England! Since this attack on the United States I am really frightened of what may happen next. Israel certainly won't be spared. America has so many enemies, and these have become Israel's enemies too, because of America's long-standing unilateral policy based on financial self-interest.

After what happened in Manhattan in September 2001 it is time that America and Europe faced up to certain mistakes that were made in their foreign policy, especially in relation to the Middle East. Actually, I think Europe can do this sooner than the United States. America is still suffering from shock and still has not admitted that its foreign policy could explain what has happened – not that this would justify it, of course.

America has not promoted democracy in Arab countries.

Take Kuwait, for example, or Saudi Arabia. These countries have no democracy, so why does America support them? Only for the reason that it wants to control the oil reserves that exist there. That is our tragedy: sources of energy have to be protected at any cost, even if it means sacrificing an entire nation.

George Bush was not really promoting a crusade. He was committing the same crime as that which was committed against his country. Indeed, his real crime was to have used the word 'crusade' for a war that has nothing to do with Christianity. The Crusades were one of the worst crimes in Christian history. By using the term, Bush justified himself for killing Muslims in the Middle East. What a disappointment! I knew his father personally, and I did not imagine he could become such an empty-headed president. Americans felt they had no choice. They had received such a blow that they felt it their duty to back their President. I was in tears when I saw the two planes destroy the Twin Towers. I immediately wrote to the American Ambassador to Israel, offering him our blood. He replied in a letter of warm appreciation. But the tragedy was that the President of a great power like America was thinking only of military force. One day it may come back to haunt him.

There were representatives of 160 countries in the Twin Towers, a symbol of economic globalization, of the economic governance of the planet. Of course, there is nothing to be said in favour of what happened. Hi-jacking planes, using men and women as hostages, killing them – all that is horrifying. To crash a plane full of human beings, innocent human victims, into a building is not just a crime, it is the act of a perverted and diabolical intelligence. It was apocalyptic. And today, what is the lesson to be drawn from this odious act? The only real security available to the rich countries will come, not from getting ready to make war, but from re-establishing justice and helping those in poverty. The poorest countries themselves should also help each other so as to take part in a process of development which would gain the respect of richer nations and so give them self-respect. With the losses caused by these attacks (estimated to be more than $100 billion), one could transform the situation of many developing countries. If this money could be used for humanitarian purposes, I would want to give a tenth of it to Afghanistan for food, agricultural equipment and everything that country needs for economic development. After that we would not see many terrorists in Afghanistan. Even if some were left, they would keep quiet and have no power to do damage to others. Good can be as contagious as evil, so long as it is done with the same strength of conviction. Instead of trying to take vengeance on my brother who has harmed me, I would go and help him to do some good.

Some peasant wisdom

Let me tell you a nice story about the love of two brothers. One was married, the other was a bachelor. They were harvesting together and putting their sheaves in the middle of the field to separate the straw from the corn. The one who was married said to himself, 'My poor brother! He has no wife or children. Who will look after him in his old age?' So every night he would take some of his sheaves of corn and place them on his brother's heap. In the morning, when he looked at his own sheaves, nothing had changed, they were all there as before – a real mystery. As for the bachelor brother, he was saying to himself, 'My poor brother! He has a wife and children. Who will help him to meet his needs? I am going to take some of my sheaves and put them with his.' So every night he went and put some sheaves of corn on his brother's heap. But when he came back in the morning he found his own heap just as big, and in some perplexity asked himself, 'How is this possible?' One night, when each of the brothers was carrying some sheaves to the other's, they met. 'What are you doing here?' said the married one to the bachelor. He replied, 'I am so sorry. As you are married, I thought of all that you were likely to need and so I added some of my sheaves to yours.' And the married one said, 'And I, knowing that you are a bachelor, was worried about your old age when you will have no one to help you and so I added some of my sheaves to yours.' At which they threw their sheaves on the ground and embraced each other with tears of joy.

Today I am afraid that stories like that are out of fashion. Nevertheless, peasant wisdom is still humanity's wisdom. Do we have to write a book to get Mr Bush to read stories like that? I was praying for Mr Bush sincerely, every day. He had so many responsibilities, so much power. He could have destroyed the planet if he wanted to. Given the decisions he made, I am afraid this is exactly what, indirectly, he might have done.

If Afghanistan, South Lebanon, Iran and other countries that were threatened by Bush are attacked, I believe it will be the start of a Third World War. Once it breaks out, no one will be able to stop it. Lebanon is not a home for terrorists any more than Iran, Syria or Israel. What country has no terrorists? Those who are called 'terrorists' today, are they just the enemies of the United States? We must not forget that today nuclear weapons are no longer the monopoly of just a few. A number of states possess them. America is not the only country manufacturing chemical and biological weapons. If America does not stop in time it will have made an unpardonable mistake. It must stop playing the cowboy in the Middle East and in Asia. However much military power it has, it will never solve the problem of terrorism simply by force of arms. For terrorism is a result of injustice more than of an ideology. We are no further advanced than the prophets of the Old Testament who said, 'If you want peace and security, begin by practising justice and integrity.' I repeat to everyone, to the *Herald Tribune*, the *New York Times*, to the international community, 'Try to do less talking. You are always talking about peace, but you are preparing for war. You talk about peace, but you send planes to scatter bombs and destroy countries, whole populations of men, women and children. Stop talking about peace and begin by introducing some justice and integrity in the countries where you are making war. In that way you may succeed in containing terrorism.'

I do not have to put myself in the shoes of Europe or America to make a conscientious judgement. I have many American friends for whom I feel respect and affection. I have learnt a great deal from them, particularly important qualities like generosity, kindness and humility. There is a mysterious gap between these groups of individuals and their foreign policy. Americans have a short memory – perhaps this is a reason for the gap. They claim that their country is the most civilized, the most democratic of the planet, but they forget that their civilization only exists at the cost of another, that of the Indians whom they decimated by millions.

I have lived in the United States, in Chicago. For three months I taught at the McCormick seminary in Hyde Park University. Never in my life have I seen so much violence. The first piece of advice I was given was the following: 'Do you see this street? Always walk on the right hand sidewalk and never cross the road, otherwise your life will be in danger. The left hand sidewalk belongs to the Mafia.' The city centre is the most dangerous place in the United States. In certain streets in Chicago, when you are in your car, you must close the windows and lock the doors. In Washington DC there is a murder every hour. I am sorry for the Americans who are victims of their own violence.

One thing that has always shocked me in talk about Israel and Palestine is the way an exception is always used to accuse the majority. If a young Palestinian, reduced to despair by losing his mother and father, buys a bomb in Israel (not being able to in Palestine – how absurd all this is!) and places it in an empty field, the immediate reaction of the international press is 'Palestinian terrorists' or 'these Palestinian terrorists': they use the exception to condemn the majority. When Israel invaded Lebanon in 1982 and 10,000 Lebanese were killed, some west-erners said to me, 'Father Chacour, have some common sense: 300,000 Israelis were against the invasion, they even protested in the streets of Tel Aviv.' Another instance of the exception being used to justify a reprehensible action! The occupation of Lebanon lasted more than 30 years and created thousands of victims. I don't approve of either the Israeli occupation or of Hezbollah, but I use this example to underline the atrocity which consists in judging a community on the basis of an individual act which has nothing to do with it. When the Ministry of Foreign Affairs in Oklahoma was destroyed by a terrorist attack, a Palestinian was suspected immediately. But it turned out that the author of the attack was neither a Palestinian nor an Arab but an American with blond hair the colour of corn! No one apologized. But it is wrong to caricature a whole people. There are good and bad people everywhere. A single wicked person is not enough to stigmatize all the others who are good.

Before taking action one has to calculate the power one disposes of and then set limits to the operation. One must have the humility not to pretend to be able to solve the problem. Of course one must be ready to act, but at one's own level. God, I am sure, wants us to persevere if we are to succeed. As a peasant in a village I can influence perhaps 200 or 300 people. Someone who publishes books may influence several hundred or several thousand people. We have to be humble enough to realize that we cannot influence the whole world. Indeed it is this humility that enables us to make progress. Each of us is a mixture of great and small. Some have wider influence because they have a larger circle. Thus, Mr Bush could launch a war. The problem was not that he had so much power. The problem was the way he used the power God had given him.

8

Some Autobiography

I was ordained priest in 1965 after having spent six years in Paris at Saint Sulpice and the Sorbonne. I learnt a great deal during this time, and it was one of the best times of my life. It was there that I became conscious of my nationality as a Palestinian and of my non-recognition by the West.

I remember one Christmas Eve when a French family, who have been friends ever since, invited me to spend Christmas with them. I had no idea why they had invited me. As we were going in to the meal I realized I was not the only guest. There were about 30 people there, including some Jews. This is how our host introduced me: 'This is Elias Chacour, a Jew born in Bethlehem.' I replied, 'No, Sir, I am not a Jew and I was not born in Bethlehem.' 'Be quiet,' he said, 'and accept what I say.' 'But it isn't the truth!' I replied.

After six years of study in Paris I came back to Galilee and my ordination took place in Nazareth. A fortnight later my bishop said to me, 'Elias, go into this village for a month, and then we shall see where to send you permanently.' I was too young to protest and ask questions, so I said yes to the bishop and went to the village. Like most bishops he had a short memory. In the end the month became 36 years.

When I arrived in this small parish, I imagined that the life that awaited me would be like the one I had had in Paris. I found I had nothing whatever except what I had brought with me. For six months I slept in a Volkswagen. The bishop knew nothing about it. Indeed, I was pretty sure he did not want to know. In the village where he had sent me there was nothing – no water, no electricity. We had water just twice a week, which I learnt how to manage with. I could have fallen into despair. But I followed the example of all the Palestinians who, despite their sufferings and the constant injustices they have to bear, continue to hope and to look ahead towards finding some spring in the desert. Remember what Saint-Exupéry said: 'Somewhere in the desert there is always a source of fresh water.'

So I embarked on several projects. The best of them was the one for holiday camps. I wanted to organize these camps because the children had nothing to do during the two and a half months of summer holidays. For my first camp I had allowed for 500 children. On the first day I was confronted by 1,128! I either had to turn some of them away, which was impossible, or cut down on the more expensive activities – which is what I decided to do. I suggested they should sleep under the olive trees – an innocent idea, sleeping under olive trees – though in fact not quite so innocent: every day I reminded them that these olive trees were 2,000 years old. Every day I told them that these olive trees had been planted by their ancestors. And I asked them if they knew what that meant. And then I added, 'What it means is that your own roots are still older than the roots of these olive trees that have been here for over 2,000 years.'

For the most recent camp there were 5,000 children, coming from 30 Galilean villages. My Christian readers do not need reminding that what was needed was a miracle – the feeding of the 5,000! At that moment I really needed a feeding miracle. Indeed I needed more. I needed the miracle three times a day for three weeks! At that time I spent much time in prayer – something I do not have time for now. So I went on retreat for a whole day to discover how to procure a miracle for feeding the multitudes. In the end I found it. That very evening I brought together all these children's mothers in a series of meetings. There were 30 mothers' meetings in the children's 30 villages. We asked each group of mothers to send us each day ten of their number with some bread. Every day we found we had 300 mothers making sandwiches and supplying drinks for our 5,000 children. You might say, 'Father Chacour, you must have a wonderful Christian community there!' To which my reply is, 'Yes, it is true, I have a wonderful Christian community, apart from the fact that three quarters of these mothers are Muslim.' We Christians do not have a monopoly of the Holy Spirit. Other people can do just as much good as we can. Indeed they often do more. We have to find the presence of God in each one and play down our religious, political or ethnic affiliation.

Another thing that has happened is the opening of children's playgrounds and public libraries in a number of villages. Since there is no electricity in our village, and therefore no television or radio, what is there to do apart from reading? Two years after the opening of the library in Ibillin, children are ashamed to go out into the street without a book in their hands. They have to be able to say, 'I am reading. I have a friend – my book.'

When Christ said, 'Help the poor, free the prisoners' he was talking politics. Which was his party? He had his own party! Woe to a priest who becomes known as a politician rather than as a man of God. If he still wears a cassock he should take it off and become whatever he likes, but he should not be an ecclesiastic. I have several times had a chance to become a member of the Knesset. On one of them my bishop urged me to stand for election. I said to him, 'My friend, I believe a little sermon in a church where there is only one old lady is worth more than a thousand speeches in the Knesset.' When he asked me why, I replied, 'Because in the Knesset I would have to speak for my party, whereas in the church I am able to say to my enemies: come and share, come and take advantage, come to forgive and to be forgiven – and that is not the language of politics.'

I well know that some members of the Israeli government are hostile to me. I tell them that they are to be pitied for not allowing themselves to be loved. I wish them no harm. Indeed, on the contrary, I simply long for them to make an effort to make a qualitative change in their relationship with us. I don't want to be tolerated, I want to be accepted. I don't want to be a stranger in my own house.

When I began building the school I was Israel's *bête noire*. My reputation with the government was very bad indeed. I was regarded as anti-Israeli, which has always been untrue. What *is* true is that I always demanded to be able to return to my village – but I will never use violence to achieve what I want.

Little by little the members of the government began to get to know me, particularly because of the support I received from certain international institutions – I was awarded honours such as the Legion of Honour, the Peace Prize of the Methodist Church, doctorates from six universities of world stature, the Japanese Niwano Prize, the Marcel-Rudolf Prize for Toleration in Strasbourg . . . As a result, our Jewish friends began to think twice before accusing me, and I think I can say that they have now understood that I intend no violence and wish them no harm. The climax of this came with Shimon Peres's visit a few years ago. What he said to me was, 'For 20 years we thought of you as an enemy of Israel, but what we have found is a friend who likes to speak the truth to us even if it is difficult for us to accept it. That is why, from now on, if you need any help, do not go to the Americans, but come and see me. I will be your ambassador.'

I must also tell the story of my house. Before I lived there I was staying in a tiny and very damp room. One day I had asthma, and there was staying with me a priest from Kentucky, who said to me, 'Listen, Father Chacour. I am an old priest, I am 75 years old, and I come to Israel twice a year to meditate, to read the Bible and to have some peace. I wanted to buy a room in Jerusalem, but they were too expensive. There is also the problem of staircases, and when I am outside I see all these Jews and Arabs who show their hatred for each other with stones and weapons – none of that helps me to meditate or pray. In short, I am not satisfied. My friends have often advised me to come and see you . Could you let me have a room?' I replied, 'But of course, Father. Take whichever you like.' He asked me how much he owed me, and I said that as I received everything for nothing I would let him have it for the same. He asked me where he could eat and I replied that he could either eat with me or on his own, since his room had a kitchenette. He said all that was fine but he had a real problem in going up and down stairs several times a day. I told him that was the only thing I could do nothing about. 'If I had a house, I would have given you the best room,' I said. Surprised, he replied, 'Why haven't you got a house?' I told him, 'Because it is not one of my priorities. If I had any money I would begin by building some classrooms.' He said to me, 'You are too young to understand. But you absolutely must have a house built.' He asked me how much it would cost and I said I thought $95,000 should cover it. He got up and said, 'I am off now. I am leaving you a cheque for $40,000, and each month I will send you another $10,000 until the house is built. When it is ready I shall hope to have the best room.' It did cost us $94,000. Two years later, he came back to see his room. When he came in and saw the shower, and the bed, he began to weep. 'I am now 77,' he said, 'and this is the last time I shall come to Israel. You can use this room for your friends. I am greatly encouraged by it. Take advantage of it and enjoy it.' At that he went away. For three months he was in hospital, and died at Christmas 2000. A month after his death I had a visit from an old lady, who asked me if I knew where Father Chacour lived. I said I did, and she asked if she could visit the house. When I showed it to her she asked if it was the same house as Father Robert had had built for Father Chacour. I told her it was, and when she saw the room that was meant for him, she burst into tears. Then she asked me, 'Can I see Father Chacour?'

I said, 'Yes, certainly.'

'When?'

'Straight away.'

'Where is he?'

'Here in front of you. I am Father Chacour.'

'I am Father Robert's sister. I came to see what he did for you. I am so glad. Here is a cheque for $10,000 for your school and to thank you for having accepted this house. It was his greatest consolation in the last years of his life.'

There are many other stories like that which I could tell. One day a man called Jim Ryan arrived at the school when I was away. He was looked after by the headmaster, who for two hours was questioned by him about my work and my future plans. When I got back, Mr Ryan was waiting for me. He said, 'God has sent me to see you.'

'Oh,' I said, 'how is he?'

'No,' he said, 'God is not joking, this is quite serious. He has sent me to ask whether you need anything.'

'Please greet him from me and tell him I don't need anything.'

'Don't you even need any money? He sent me to give you some.'

'I don't want your money. I don't know you. I am afraid that you may be wanting to give me this money simply to have a quiet conscience. I feel there is something fishy about this.'

'How can you say that?'

'If you have nothing but money to give me, you must be terribly poor!'

'But what else do you want?'

'If we become friends and come to terms with each other, then perhaps this gift will mean something. If not, I would rather you went away and took your money with you.'

We went on talking for an hour and a half, and became friends. When he went he left a cheque for $100,000 on the table. Over three months he gave us $240,000. Thanks to this we were able to complete the sports hall. It turned out that this person was one of the five biggest building contractors in the United States.

There are also many stories that have nothing to do with money – stories of friendship. The fact that I am still a priest is thanks to the friendship I have received all over the world.

One of the most moving days in my life was 28 February 1972 when the municipality of Ibillin made me its first honorary citizen. Another was 1 September 1982, the date on which I opened the school. After nine months of struggle and 18-hour working days my dream was finally becoming reality. At the start we had 80 students. Today we have 4,500 (see note on page 42). These have been moments of great happiness. But I have done nothing to deserve them. They are due to the grace of God and to the generosity of friends throughout the world.

One day, when I was in my office, someone knocked at the door. 'Good morning, I have come from Australia. I am the Archbishop of Melbourne.' I replied, 'And I am the parish priest of Ibillin in Galilee. Do come in.'

'I have come to see you because I want to get to know you and give you some help.' It turned out that when he went to Australia he distributed some thousands of copies of my book, *Blood Brothers*. I became great friends with this Anglican Archbishop of Melbourne, David Penman. Each time he came to Palestine he never failed to come and see me, and it was truly a joy to have him with us. He invited me to Melbourne to open the Anglican Synod.

Two years after this invitation was given I took a plane again, this time to Sydney. When I arrived I learnt that he had died of a heart attack. I attended his funeral. The following year I received an invitation from his widow. She wanted to be ordained as a priest to honour his memory, and desired that it should be I who delivered the sermon at the ordination. This was a real problem for me, since as a Catholic priest, and a Greek Catholic at that (which means more conservative than most), I could not but think it a grave error to preach at the ordination of a woman. I prayed about it a great deal, and spent a long time trying to work out what I should do. Finally, I went and I preached. I spoke of the role of Mary in Jesus' life, and I ended with a question: 'We accept that Christ was given to us by means of a woman; why then should we not accept that a woman may give us the Eucharist? I shall be grateful to anyone who can give me the answer! Amen.'

These have been wonderful moments in my life, but there have also been some very tragic ones. There is one episode which has deeply affected my life and which I will never forget. One of my colleagues, a priest, was accused by a third party of scandalous conduct. The bishop suspended him, so that he could no longer officiate. I was disgusted by this decision, since I knew that the accusation was unfounded. I risked my own priesthood in order to defend him. After two years, somewhat craftily, I succeeded in persuading the bishop to let this priest say mass again on Easter Day. The bishop said to me, 'You will never find anyone who will allow him to do this in his church.'

'I will find someone.'

'If you can find someone I will allow it. It is not a matter of doctrine, it is a matter of the oriental instinct for revenge.'

'Are you serious, My Lord?'

'Yes.'

'Well then, I have found someone.'

'And who is that?'

'It is me. I will let him take my place.'

'But then where will you go to say mass?'

'Each day I shall go to a different church and concelebrate the mass with the priest there. I shall go to preach the good news.'

'What good news?'

'The good news that the bishop and Father F. have made it up together.'

He could not refuse, and Father F. took my place in the parish. On Easter Sunday, after having celebrated mass in another parish with another parish priest, I came straight back to my own. Father F. was still celebrating the Eucharist. His mother was seated at the front, and, seeing me come in, threw herself on my neck, thanking me with tears for what I had done. Every time I think of this episode tears come to my eyes. I had wanted to get my brother back when others wanted him to disappear. He had been imprisoned in a dark cell, and had nearly been deprived of his priesthood because he raised objections to some of our people who were politically too powerful to be able to act justly. They sensed a rival in him who must be got rid of at all costs. He on his part certainly gave them reasons: he was a defender of the Catholic faith! Just think of all the crimes that have been committed in the name of this faith and of this Church whose Lord and Master would not break a reed and who refused to condemn a prostitute! He could only love and forgive: Father, forgive them, for they do not know what they do.

The saddest of these episodes was the day I had to take my bishop to court. It was in 1978. The Secretary General of the United Nations had insisted that I should go to Cambodia to report on the situation and suggest ways of making peace between the Khmer and the Khmer Rouge. I was accompanied by the Dalai Lama and Elie Wiesel. We visited several cities, including Phnom Penh. I came back excited by my visit, because I found it to be fertile territory for reconciliation and peace.

When I got back, I checked the accounts of the school and noticed that there was nothing in the bank. It was the end of the month, and we had to pay the salaries of 69 teachers.

Thinking that the government grants had not been paid, I telephoned the Ministry at once. They replied, 'But, Mr Chacour, we paid you at the beginning of the month.' I asked them how our account could possibly be empty. They replied, 'You must have a short memory. You wrote us a letter informing us you were changing your account.' I said, 'It must have been my secretary who looked after that and she has forgotten to make a copy for me. Could you send me a copy of the letter?' They faxed me a copy. I found that my former archbishop had used my name to sign some letters from the archbishop's office, asking for the account to be transferred to him personally. I went to see him and said, 'My Lord, you ought to have consulted me before making this transfer.' He replied, 'I have some debts and I need the money. You must do what you can.' 'But the money you have taken does not belong to me. This is about the bread of the poor, the salaries of 69 teachers. You can't confiscate that.' He replied, 'That doesn't matter, I am the bishop and it is up to me.' I tried in every way I could to make him see it, I told him that this was bad, immoral, unjust – but it was no use.

I went to see the Apostolic Delegate in Jerusalem, who said to me, 'You owe obedience to your bishop. Let him do what he wants, he will have to render account to God.' I replied, 'But I have to render account to my teachers. They are the poor of my country, they must be respected. If there is nothing you can do, I shall have to go to court.' He would not listen, and just said, 'Do what seems best to you; but you must obey your bishop.' I went to see the Patriarch's Vicar General in Jerusalem and told him the whole story. He asked me, 'Would you like me to telephone the bishop and ask him to explain the reasons why he has done this?' I answered, 'If you have no authority over him, I have no need of your pity.' He began to weep, and said, 'I don't know why the bishop does stupid things like this.' In short, he did nothing. Then I went to the Ministry of Education where there were Jews, not Christians. I told the head of the department what had happened. He told me to go to court. I asked him if the ministry's lawyer could take on our case, and he replied that he would be at our disposal. I went back to the bishop and pleaded with him to reverse his decision. He replied that I was being arrogant. I offered to resign the following June, to which he replied, 'Why not resign at once?' I was outraged, and said to him, 'You do not seem to understand people's language when they are showing you kindness and concern. Is force the only thing you understand?'

So I went to the court in Jerusalem and lodged my appeal. I obtained the document I needed, which gave him the choice of returning the money to us or going to prison. When he saw it, the bishop asked me what the document was. I said, 'It is a court order that the Bishop of Galilee should return the money or else go to prison.' He asked me, 'Who is responsible for this court order?' I replied, 'The little parish priest of Ibillin.' He summoned his secretary, and then his lawyer. Both of them told him it was serious and he would have to give back the money. The bishop said to me, 'You are getting powerful, my parish priest!' I replied, 'It is because you are weak in the face of money, my Lord Bishop!' I was assured that the bishop would never ever again demean himself by touching the school's money.

That was not the end of the surprises in store for me. When I got back home I felt utterly miserable. Two police officers of the Israeli Security Services were waiting for me. When I asked what they wanted, they replied, 'How much longer are you going to oppose your bishop?' I asked them whether that was a matter for the state. They replied, 'We need to know everything.' I asked one of them whether he had a wife. He said he had, and when I put the same question to his colleague he also said yes. Then I asked them if they had children. One of them said he had, and I asked him if all was well. He replied that it was not: he was on the point of a divorce. From then on he completely forgot what he had come about. We talked about his family problems for a good hour, and he then agreed to come and see me with his wife. Later on he confessed to me that it was on the orders of the bishop that they had come, and they were supposed to give me a rough time. I telephoned the bishop and told him that his emissaries had shown a great deal more humanity than the man who had sent them, and that this was unworthy of him. He pretended not to understand. I went on seeing the policeman as well as his wife. And the divorce never happened.

Despite this sad story I did not stop loving and respecting this bishop. But I cannot forget what he did to me. I am prepared to go to any lengths when it is a matter of defending the poor. In the last analysis, the one thing which kept my relationship with my bishop intact was my wish to remain in communion with him or under his jurisdiction, and certainly not to abandon him in his humiliation. This same bishop came to see me the following year. He wanted me to become the chief administrator of the diocese, and to be made an archimandrite. I refused and suggested he found someone else. I explained that I would never be able to place my confidence in him. He tried to persuade me to accept, but it was a waste of time. A few months later he resigned and went away. Today we are still trying to repair the financial damage he did to the diocese. He sold lands that belonged to the Church, and offered tenancies to Jewish associations for 1,008 years. He signed contracts with workmen who knew about his misdeeds, and these contained a special clause entitling them to an indemnity of 500 per cent of their salary if they were dismissed. And much more of the same.

Instead of feeling indignation and rejection, I began to realize the full force of the last course in Canon Law which we followed in Paris. Our instructor told us, 'I know that you don't care for Canon Law. But if you are going to work in our Church you must remember that in that holy body which is the Church there exists absolutely everything except what is metaphysically impossible.' I have discovered that what he said is absolutely true. And I am not shocked by it. It has made me even more determined to go forward. I love my Church as I love my mother. I do not want her to die, I want her to live. I am ready to give her everything, because I have no better way of doing some good.

This is the truth which has given me the resources to keep alive my relationship with my present bishop, who is one of my closest friends, a man of God, open-hearted and transparently honest. I am glad to be alive, very glad. It was a hard choice that I made in following this path, a choice I have to make afresh every day. I have nothing to regret. I have often had to face up to dreadful and depressing situations, but I have never lost sight of the fact that carrying the cross is a day's work, a long day's work. It is Good Friday all the time, the day of the crucifixion. But that day will always be followed without fail by the Sunday of the resurrection, and that day will have no end. If one has to pass through the Friday of the crucifixion, it may be unpleasant but, my goodness, it is worthwhile! At the end of the tunnel there is a light, there is the empty tomb, there is the resurrection. That is our destiny.

One day I felt that I had had enough of the quarrels and absurd jealousies that go on inside the church. I had had enough of the political pressures we were subjected to. I wanted to go away and hear nothing more about priests and Palestinians and Jews. That is why, as I have said already, I went away to Switzerland. I thought I could be happy there, but I did not find what I was looking for. The problem was within myself. It was myself I had to accept first. I am not an important person, I have no influence, I am not a saint or a scholar or a superman. I am first and foremost a Galilean peasant. The family I come from is poor, but it knows the value of love and sharing. I am well aware that everything I possess today I owe to my friends and to the support of many people all over the world. Anyone who is afraid of me, thinking that I have power, is quite wrong. I am a man like other men. If I am strong, it is because of my ability to persevere. I never give up. This is one of God's gifts. God simply makes use of me as he thinks best. He does not need me but, for my part, I am grateful for everything he gives me. I am not indispensable, but I am irreplaceable, as we all are. Each of us is unique.

The mistake you make in the West is that you always want to distinguish between the person and the action. You are inclined to believe that thinking is for the intellect and loving is for the heart. What I would like you to do is love with your mind and think with your heart. We don't only love with our hearts, we love with our minds too. I would like you to bring heart and mind together again. God is not stupid. He could have saved us simply by saying, 'I am saving you, I forgive you.' There was no need for him to become incarnate, to be crucified. He could have saved us with no effort. But no, he decided otherwise. He wanted there to be a better world. 'Love one another as I have loved you. Minister to one another as I have ministered to you. I have washed your feet and kissed them.' That is God's way of saving us. It was not something he needed to do, it was because we needed it. What he said was, 'If you want to be saved, then take up your cross and follow me. You are quite free not to take it up, you are quite free not to follow me – but then you cannot be saved.' We must not try to change places with him. If you walk in front of the Lord all you will see is your own shadow. If you walk behind him, then you will see the light, then you will see him as he is. We depend on him. This is the way he has chosen – but he has left us free.

As for those who do not know God, the question was put long ago to St Paul, who replied, 'Do not judge them. They will be judged according to their own law. God may have made it possible for them not to know him, but that does not mean that he has destined them to being banished from his presence.'

9

Jesus in the Gospels: A Galilean Reading

Christ never delivered the Sermon on the Mount the way it is written and neatly arranged in the gospel. It was the apostles who reconstructed it and wrote down Christ's sayings. When you read the Bible you must remember that the Bible is also reading you. The first thing you read about in the Bible is yourself. In the same way, when you read the beatitudes, you are first of all reading about Jesus' disciples. They are telling you how they have seen Christ. What does the Lord mean to us? What did he mean to them? In order to tell us they memorized some of Christ's words and put them together for us in the Sermon on the Mount. If we are to understand this sermon, we have to put it back in its context: Galilee in the time of Christ. And anyway the Sermon on the Mount is not a sermon on a mountain. There was no mountain. From a distance, you might imagine it being as high as Mont Blanc. But this is quite wrong. We are not talking about a mountain, but about the side of the Lake of Tiberias. Moreover the place is below sea level, it is the lowest place on earth. It is because Christ sat on this 'mount' that it seems so high to us. It has the height given to it by Christ.

For me, a Galilean and a Christian, the Sermon on the

Mount is not confined to three chapters of Matthew's Gospel. The Sermon on the Mount is nothing less than Jesus himself. Christ and the Sermon are one and the same. I like to read the sermon in the context of Capernaum. Christ had to leave Nazareth because the inhabitants lacked faith. All they were interested in was his miracles, so that they could say he was one of them. They wanted to be able to boast in front of the inhabitants of other towns and villages who came to do their shopping in Nazareth. Things are much the same today, nothing has really changed. The people of Nazareth still want visitors – tourists – and to attract them they need something they can talk about which is different from anywhere else. At that time they did not believe. They had no need to believe. They simply wanted to do business and they found Christ useful for the purpose. Whereas he, seeing how incredulous the people of Nazareth were, decided to leave the town for good.

Christ's miracles were not intended to make us believe. It is the other way round: because you have believed, you will now see proof of God's mercy. It is your faith that saves you. 'Woman,' he says, 'go in peace. Your faith has saved you.' Soon after that, he sees the faith of those who carried in the paralysed man and let him down through the roof, and he says to the man, 'Your sins are forgiven.' And won't he say to the centurion, 'Nowhere have I seen such faith, no, not in Israel'? And what does he say to Mary, the sister of Lazarus? 'Only believe, and you will see the power of God. Blest are those who have not seen and yet have believed' – and so on.

So Jesus leaves Nazareth and goes to Cana, where he is invited to a wedding with his mother. In oriental culture it is not done to leave behind one's friends when one is invited to a celebration. Jesus is an oriental. So he invites all his friends to the wedding in Cana. As a good member of the family, he arrives several days before the wedding, to eat and drink and sing and dance with them. Mary can certainly sing. She can also improvise a song, as she did once before when she visited Elizabeth. What she sang there, with joy in her heart, was 'My soul doth magnify the Lord . . . He has done great things for me, for holy is his name.' My mother can make up a song in the same way. She sang when I was made a priest, she sang when I was made first citizen of Ibillin, she has sung for all the good moments in my life. It has been a kind of blessing. It was also a prayer to the Lord that he would grant still more of his grace and shower still more of his blessings upon me.

Anyway, Mary and her son are there at Cana with his friends. They are fishermen. They know all about preparing and eating fish. They know how to drink without letting alcohol affect them, which is what they have been doing for the three days before the wedding. But it happens that Mary, who is busy in the kitchen, notices that the wine is running out and that there will certainly not be enough for the rest of the festivities. I remember the wedding of my elder brother. My father had thought about the wine for a whole year beforehand. Everything had been thought of. If, by an evil chance, there had been any shortage of food and drink, it would have caused a scandal.

Mary was in the kitchen and realized the shame that the family would incur if the wine ran out. So she went to find Jesus and ask him if he could do something about it. I think what she went to say to him was, 'Tell your disciples to drink a bit less, because the wine has begun to run out – which could cause a scandal.' Christ then looked at his mother and said, 'Woman, why are you coming to me about it?' (the word 'woman', in this context, was a term of respect, meaning 'mother of the living'), 'What do you want? It is not my time yet.' And what did Mary do? She paid no attention to what Jesus said to her. He was her son, he had to obey her. She said to him, 'Do something.' She then turned to the servants and told them to do whatever Jesus said. Jesus knew he must respect his mother, but he also had to think of his friends. And so he turned the water into wine so that they could keep on enjoying themselves.

The news got round. People came in large numbers to see the man who had changed the water meant for ablutions into wine. Jesus did not leave at once. He had to stay after the wedding to be with the family. The wedding couple left and the house was emptied. Then Jesus got up and left as well. Everyone wanted to escort him to the edge of the village, for he had become a celebrity.

In the distance a cloud of dust was forming. It was steadily coming closer. It was a centurion with his troop of 100 soldiers coming to the gates of Cana. Surely he must have been coming for some important reason? When he arrived in front of Jesus he dismounted and asked him, 'Please do something. My daughter is dying. Say the word and she will be cured.' People were crowding round Jesus. This was a Roman, one of the occupiers, coming to implore Christ to do something for his daughter. But the centurion went on, 'No, you must not come under my roof. Only say the word and my daughter will be cured. In some ways I am just like you, I have 100 soldiers under my orders. I say to one, "Come", and he comes, to another, "Go", and he goes. For your part, you have life and death under your orders. You can say to life, "Come", and it will come, just as you can say to death, "Go", and it will go. Just say the word, and that will be enough.'

Why did the centurion not want Jesus to come home with him? Because he did not want to humiliate him. When you become someone's guest that person becomes your host and you have to do what he says. The centurion said to Jesus, 'I am not worthy for you to come into my home, I cannot tell you what to do, because you are greater than me.' Just at this moment Jesus shouted out, 'Who touched me?' Peter turned to him and said, 'But, Lord, everyone is touching you, everyone is elbowing forward to touch you.' But Jesus said, 'No, no; someone touched me and I felt power going out of me.' Then a woman came up. She realized she could not keep up the pretence any longer in the eyes of someone like Jesus. She said, 'Lord, it is I who touched you, and I am cured.' Then Christ said to her, 'Your faith has saved you, go in peace.'

The centurion, who had not forgotten why he had come, went on beseeching Jesus, saying, 'Are you going to cure my daughter?' And Christ replied, 'Be it done to you according to your faith. Go in peace, your daughter is cured.'

Jesus' reputation had by now spread to all the villages around. When he got to Capernaum he went to Peter's house and stayed there. The house was full of people, who were pressing round to see Jesus. It had become impossible to go in or out. In the town there was a paralytic. Four members of his family decided to bring him to Christ to be healed. But how could they get into the house where there were already so many people?

They did what I did when I was small. There was a place where they stored straw for the animals. At harvest time they threw it in through a hole in the roof. In summer, they blocked up the hole with pieces of wood so that birds and snakes could not get in. I and my brother Atallah used to like to climb on the roof and jump into this store holding hands. Each time we did it we prayed to the prophet Elijah to protect us as we jumped. So it was through the roof that these people were able to let the paralytic down into Peter's house. They found themselves in a room where the door was shut because it was never used. On the other side of this door sat the guest of honour; he had been given this place because he would not be disturbed there. So when the paralytic's family opened this door which was never opened, they found themselves in front of Jesus. Christ said not a word to the paralytic, he simply looked at him. He saw the faith of those who had brought him to him. That was enough for him. He cured the paralytic.

At Capernaum there was a large crowd, even larger than the crowd that gathers to see the Pope. They came from Judea, from Samaria, from all over Galilee, from Tyre and Sidon. They all wanted to see this extraordinary man.

Towards five o'clock in the morning Peter got up to get breakfast for his master. That morning he could not find him. But Peter knew where he would be. He went out of the house where the crowd was already gathered, climbed the slope of the hill beside the Lake of Tiberias and found the Lord sitting there. Peter knew that when Jesus was sitting alone like this he was speaking with his Father. Isn't that what prayer truly is?

The mount Jesus was sitting on was no more than a little hill. Anyone could have climbed it. When Jesus saw Peter with the apostles and the whole crowd, he said, 'These are sheep without a shepherd. Come, draw near.' He wanted people to come near to him so that he would be at one with them. That is why he ended up by giving us his body and his blood so that we should become Christ and he should become man. I can well imagine Peter and the disciples sitting round Jesus, and behind them the Pharisees, the politicians, and the people whose job it was to take back to the authorities a report of what Jesus was saying. There were also some sick people. Then Jesus began to speak to the people, his friends, the sheep without a shepherd. He saw himself as their shepherd, the good shepherd who knows his sheep and is known by them. 'Come to me, all you who are in trouble and I will relieve you. That is what it means to love and be loved. That is reunion and reconciliation. That is how the father is reconciled and reunited with his prodigal son . . . Come, draw near, sit close to me. As close as possible, don't be afraid, be confident: it is I. Peace be with you. I have come to give you joy, and I want your joy to be perfect. *Shlomo alaikhum, shalom aleikhem, assalam aleikoum.*'

10

The Road to Peace: A Meditation

The Lord was saying, 'Get up, choose where you are going and go! If you are hungry and thirsty for justice, get up and get your hands dirty.' When we think of Christ, we realize that he got much more than his hands dirty for us. He got dirty all over so that we could have peace, real peace, the peace that for his part he never lost, least of all when he was on the cross. This interior peace never left him, and when he saw the wretches who were crucifying him he said, 'Father, forgive them for they know not what they do.'

After the eight beatitudes we read, 'You are the light of the world.' You cannot hide a city that is built on a hill and you do not put your light under a bushel. No, your actions should be visible to all for the glory of God the Father. When I look at the history of Christianity, I really have to confess that on many occasions the Christian world has behaved badly. Again and again Christians have wanted to be distinguished and famous instead of using the light in such a way that people can see past us and discover their saviour. I can hear the Third World, the non-Christian world, saying, Yes, you Christians, you may be the light, but please dim your headlights, you are blinding us with your brightness, we can no longer see the way, we cannot see where we are going because of your blinding light. The cradle of your Lord was not something blinding. It was humble and alluring. We feel comfortable with it when we are with your Lord at the beginning of the story. Allow us to see him. Dim your lights.

The light needs to be softer. There are two things that blind us: darkness, and light that is too bright. Jesus ends by saying, 'You are the salt of the earth.' In Aramaic there is another text that says, 'You are the salt of the earth. If the salt goes astray, what good is the rest?' These words have a deep meaning. They show that Christ did not come to teach us a new kitchen recipe. He took the salt, this ingredient that gives taste to our food, and of which we must take just a pinch, otherwise our food becomes uneatable – he took the salt, and said to his disciples, 'You must disappear into society so that it finds flavour in the dish that is before it. You are not to be a landmark. You have got to be the condiment which makes it possible to taste and enjoy the food. You must be the way that leads to God.'

You who are poor in spirit, get on your way, do something. It is you who will be able to understand the beatitudes. The poor in spirit are those who have emptied themselves so as to be filled with God. You know that the labour is lost if it is not God who builds the house.

The pure in heart, they will see God. They will learn to see him and make room for him in their own soul and their own body, just as they will see him in the soul and the face of their neighbour. God is present in the cosmos, or rather, the cosmos is present in God. God embraces it and sustains it. God is to be seen in the little people, whether they are little in age, in physique, in importance, in ethical and moral stature. This is where we see God in his creatures. And we must not forget to see God in ourselves. Is not each one of us the most beautiful thing that God has created? 'I am black but comely' – beauty radiates from within us and gives beauty to our colour, be it black or white.

It is children who are pure in heart. They can only say yes—yes, or no—no. They add nothing to make it sound true. They do not pretend they know what they do not know. They are quick to say they are hungry when they feel it. When they eat, they accept their food as a gracious gift and a gracious offer. They don't play tricks, they are incapable of being hypocrites. Their life is for play, but not for playing a part. Their games are real to them, but they don't pretend to be something they are not. They know how to ask to be forgiven, and they are ready to forgive. Taking revenge is something they always dream of, but never do. The pure in heart are the ones who are close to God, who are God's intimates. It is Mary, the mother of Jesus, who should be the model for the pure in heart. Think of her song of wonder at all God has done for her: 'My soul doth magnify the Lord . . . and holy is his name.' The reason why Mary is called blessed by all nations is the Holy Name of the Lord. She knows that whatever greatness she has comes from the Lord.

Those of you who are humble, you will inherit the earth. Not some other earth, but this one. Not some other Planet Earth, but our own, the true Earth, the one for which the chosen people has been on the march for 40 years. We are speaking of the Promised Land, which is not just physical land but is a spiritual land which neither thieves nor moths can destroy. It is the humble who will inherit the Promised Land. The proud of this world may control the land but they will not inherit it. It is the humble and the pure in heart who will be judged worthy to return to the Promised Land. It is they who will be brought back into paradise, into the garden of Eden, where they will live in the presence of God. It is they who will know how to win over and be won over by God. It will be a return to the true Land which is not a geographical space but a fellowship, the source of life: the presence of God.

Mary was poor in spirit because she had emptied herself so as to be filled with God. And so she saw nothing in herself but what God could see in her. To see God in ourselves, in everything that we do and think, to act as if we were permanently in the divine presence – that is what it means to be pure in heart. The prophet Elijah was always repeating these words: 'As God lives before whom I stand.' For that, he was judged worthy to see the Lord in the stillness of the breeze, just as Moses met this same God in the storm and the tempest of Mount Horeb.

It is not only with our bodily eyes that we see, those two apertures in our face. To see God properly we must close our bodily eyes, which can see only what is superficial, exterior. To see clearly we must do it with the heart, with the eyes of the spirit. If you want to see clearly, shut your eyes; if you want to hear clearly, block your ears . . . What is of the earth is earthly, what is of the spirit is spiritual and eternal.

To be pure in heart we have to be poor in spirit. Only so will we become hungry and thirsty for justice. Then we shall understand the importance of commitment and risk-taking in order to bring about justice and live with integrity. Then we shall be able to bring order into our lives and our actions. We shall no longer shout 'Peace, peace!' and see nothing but war, war that goes on getting ever more horrifying. We shall stop trying to establish our security, which at the end of the day is nothing but domination and segregation masquerading as peace. We shall begin to do justly, to have moral integrity. We shall become peacemakers, makers of his Peace. And then we shall know its fruits: peace and love for all in this world, all who are in the Promised Land.

September–December 2001

Postscript

The War with Lebanon and its Aftermath

October 2006

The war ended after 34 days with no result except the destruction of thousands of buildings, the creation of a million refugees on the Lebanese side, psychological damage to countless people, the loss of many soldiers in Israel and the destabilization of the whole region. After this apocalyptic catastrophe we have returned to point zero. Surely there should have been immediate negotiations to liberate the two soldiers in return for the release of prisoners inside Israel. But no politician listened to the voice of wisdom. The result was the destructive use of military might, which, as usual, was counter-productive. Violence always breeds the same thing, more violence. There is no just war, there are just wars.

We, Jews and Palestinians, are bound up together. Instead of living together and completing each other we seem bent on destroying each other. The lack of any political, economic or military balance between the two sides has made negotiation difficult, if not impossible. One side has military superiority and a powerful lobby abroad. The other is in the midst of deprivations and despair. Nobody pays any attention to the daily tragedies inflicted on the Palestinian people after the elections. These were the 'democratic elections' demanded by the

western world. But the outcome, which was genuinely democratic, was rejected by those who had been promoting it. There
is no dream, no vision left in Israel–Palestine, and no sign of any
vision among the foreign powers. There is only one way to
follow, the way described by the Prophets revered in the three
monotheistic religions, who said, 'If you want peace and
security, pursue justice and integrity.' But none of us seems
prepared to follow it. One side wants peace and security without justice. The other side just wants justice – and neither side
has got anything of what it wants.

But we are still here, we are alive and full of hope. We are
looking for ways to find more hope and to discover sweetness
in the midst of the bitterness we experienced during this last
cruel, mad and absurd war.

9 781853 119064